3 . 00

Down the Hatch!

Down the Hatch!

Richard Ingrams & John Wells
Illustrated by Brian Bagnall

PRIVATE EYE/ANDRE DEUTSCH

Published in Great Britain by Private Eye Productions Ltd,
6 Carlisle Street, London W1

© 1985 Pressdram Ltd
Illustrations by Brian Bagnall © 1985

ISBN 233 97812 7

Printed by The Bath Press, Bath
Typeset by JH Graphics Ltd, Reading

Dear Bill,

As you may have seen in the gutter press Operation Markscram has now entered its crucial midway stage. Charlie Whackett has done his stuff and fixed the boy up with some kind of Used Car Consultancy on the fifty-third floor of a very tall greenhouse in Los Angeles, the other wing of the pincer movement being the impending wedlock with Miss Fortknox. In furtherance of the second objective, a twenty-four hour Unwanted Aliens' Visa was issued to the son and heir over the weekend and he was ferried in to Chequers along with Miss F. and an entire Texan family consisting of twin brother Ben, a six-foot bruiser in a crew cut, mother Mrs Kay Fortknox with a knee-length handbag and engaging smile, accompanied by a retinue of smiling black servants, gloomy Mexican maids and an English butler called Mr Sammy Gielgud.

Saatchis had laid on a five-line whip for the reptile corps, the thinking being, quite rightly, that if everything is made public at all stages along the grisly path, the little rascal will find it extremely difficult to wriggle out of it. Accordingly we all put our smiles on and stood out on the lawn before lunch while the greasy winos of Fleet Street stumbled against one another with their cameras, shouting impertinent remarks – most of them levelled at yours truly who was expected as usual to provide some comic relief.

My own instructions from the Boss were fairly cut and dried, i.e. to refrain from hard liquor, speak only when spoken to and avoid disparaging remarks about the son and heir, Hopalong etc. A tough assignment, I think you will agree, and my immediate thought was that I would need a couple of very stiff ones if I was to carry it out. With these under the belt I advanced on Mother F. who was admiring a portrait of Mr Gladstone at his writing table. 'Why,' she cooed, laying a hand on my arm, 'I just adore your family portraits. He looks such a jolly old boy. And he has something of Mark about the eyes.' The poor woman was plainly under the delusion that the whole bang shoot belonged to us. I was all in favour of enlightening the old bird, but I could see

Margaret was in no haste to disillusion her, part of the plan being, I should say, to impress on our Texan visitors that money was the last thing in Mark's mind in offering himself as their future son-in-law. However when Mother F. caught sight of Sailor Ted in pride of place on the first landing and exclaimed 'Now, Margaret, *that* must be your brother! What a handsome man, and what a delightful smile,' the subterfuge inevitably gave way. A hard light appeared in the Proprietor's eye and she gave our guest a brief history lesson to include an account of Chequers and the many inadequacies of its last Conservative occupant.

It was clear that the WAAF officiating with the booze had been tipped off to keep us in short supply, so after an hour and a half next to Mother F. at lunch I was pretty dazed and, unwisely as it transpired, slipped into the Butler's Pantry to solicit Boris for an Emergency Transfusion. Boris and Mr Gielgud had clearly hit it off remarkably well and the flood of anecdote and reminiscence was a good deal more entertaining than was the case next door. When I toddled back in, looking perhaps more cheerful than I should have done, the conversation had turned to the topic of Hopalong's possible re-election. You know my views on this, and I immediately trotted them out, saying that I could never understand how an old cowboy actor could be put in charge of running a country and that people over here would think it jolly odd if we had Donald Sinden as top cat. It was clear to me they had no idea who I was talking about and, though Margaret was fixing me with the gimlet eye from the other end of the table, I proceeded to my second theory, namely that he hadn't the hope of a snowball in hell if he persisted in stripping off and going for a swim looking like some halfwit from Butlin's Eventide Homes, certainly not if he combined it with holding hands with his wife. 'Look what happened to the fellow before, the peanut man who was always falling over. They soon got rid of him.' For some reason I found all this hugely amusing and it was a few moments before I realised that the company did not. 'I take it you are referring to our dear friend Jimmy Carter,' crooned Mother F. in a frostyish tone. 'Jimmy is godfather to our Ben here.' Ben nodded gravely at this and it was clear to me that I had plunged the pedal extremity into the ordure. The gamma quotient was stepped up from the head of the table and D.T. was once again reduced to a small smouldering heap of ash on the dining room chair.

However on other fronts my efforts in bringing about world peace have been more signally successful. I didn't mention it at

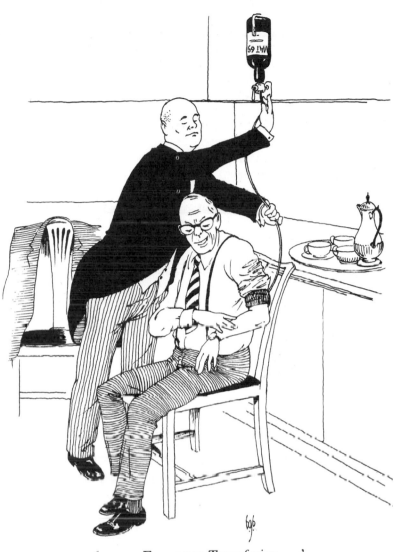

'. . . an Emergency Transfusion . . .'

the time, Mum being very much the word, but during my
stopover in Jo'burg some months back where I was doing my best
to interest the natives in Maurice's Picvid Film and Video
venture, I presented myself at a reception given by Mrs Van der
Kefferbesher and ran into their Supremo Mr Pik Botha. He
seemed to me a nice chap, quite a decent handicap, and very
sound on the Red Menace. After we'd had a few I suggested he

come up for the weekend some time to smack the prune round Huntercombe. He seemed unusually excited by this idea and accepted with alacrity. He arrives next week. Needless to say the great unwashed will be out en masse with their placards and the usual Rentamob. I have asked Brittan to round up the ringleaders as a matter of courtesy but I shouldn't think he'll do anything, knowing the cut of his jib. However I thought it was the least I could do as a host.

Do you fancy getting legless at Littlestone to celebrate my sixty-ninth? Give me a blow.

Yours in the Lord,

DENIS

10 Downing Street
Whitehall
1 JUNE 1984

Dear Bill,

Poor old Fatty Prior! You remember he got shunted off to Siberia after he'd failed to come to heel in the Cabinet. Since then he's been stewing in his own juice on the Bogside, pretty disgruntled but under the impression, I think, that he had only been sent to stand in the corner and would be back shortly. Little does he know the Boss. Early on she had put him down in her black book for cheek and once your name is marked it's the long lingering death being eaten alive by Doctor Paisley and the mad buggers in the woolly hats.

Ever since the entire prison population walked out in broad daylight some months back Fatty himself realised he hadn't a hope in hell of getting the better of the Bog-men and therefore leaped at this recent Dublin Forum idea, his thinking being that he could pass the buck down to them. In my view a very sound idea. As you and I have discovered on many a merry jaunt to the Emerald Isle they're a decent bunch of coves with their priorities right, i.e. (1) a drink, (2) another one, (3) well, Sir, you're a generous man, just a large one would do me nicely. The idea of these ruddy-nosed Left Footers massacring the Prods if they were allowed to run the whole show is manifestly ridiculous.

Margaret on the other hand has never had much time for the land of drinkers and dreamers, as you may remember from the time she walked out of the Arbutus Lodge in Cork when that very jolly dentist tried to slip a salmon down the back of her neck. Her view is that Sovereignty is Sovereignty even if it's costing us an arm and a leg every other second and that we shall sit it out if needs be till Kingdom Come and the Men of Violence recognise the superior force of our Rubber Bullet Brigade.

The result of this impasse is that Fatty is threatening to throw in the out-size bathtowel, pack his bags and go back to his pigs, saying as much on Radio Fenland, Margaret the while insisting he remains till he is sacked. He can then join the likes of Pym, Stevas, Heath etc in the little box with all the other pieces removed from the board.

The same philosophy of intransigence – you can tell it's pretty soon after breakfast when I can toss out a phrase of that complexity – marks Margaret's attitude to little Adolf Scargill. Despite the fact that the pound is going through the floor and my own gilt-edged investments like yours appear to be diminishing in value every time one opens a newspaper, the word is 'Ils ne passeront pass', as the barmy old Winco at the Royal Ancient and Hampstead Golf Club used to intone at the top of his voice every time Picarda applied for membership. Poor old MacGregor, who would be far happier in a bath chair doing the Daily Telegraph Crossword Puzzle, is under instructions not to rise to Scargill's provocations and sit it out until what is left of the coalmining industry has battered itself to death and we can get all our supplies dirt cheap from the Polak.

Last week in response to unrest in the ranks, Scargill finally deigned to come down and punch him on the nose in person. He and his Gauleiters boarded the Intercity, got tanked up on the Brown Ale and strode in to Coal House where the old boy was dozing in the sun with a tartan rug over his knees. According to Tebbit, the deputation paused only to swill down the beer and sandwiches provided and then read out a list of their demands, saying they would agree to talk if all their requirements were met as a prior condition. Whereupon Spencer Tracey opened his eyes and said sagely 'I have no comment'. The Barnsley Brigade then said this was the giddy limit, typical etc and shuffled off back to

'. . . that very jolly dentist . . .'

Euston and the buffet facilities available towards the middle of the train.

Did you realise Maurice was standing as a Euro-candidate for the Home Counties? He's discovered that putting together his overnights in Brussels plus travelling expenses, tax allowances, salary and other perks he'd be far better off than he is running PicVid, and he wouldn't have to work. The SDP were a bit chary about having him after the Sevenoaks debacle, so he's standing for the Greens, quite appropriate in view of his condition when I last saw him arriving at Harwich from the Rotarian Outing to Rotterdam.

What a blinder that was at Huntercombe! When I eventually came round I thought all my teeth had fallen out.

Yrs,

DENIS

 10 Downing Street
Whitehall
15 JUNE 1984

Dear Bill,
'The tumult and the shouting fades, ti-tum, ti-tum, ti-tum, ti-tum,' as the old song has it. I am seriously thinking of going on the wagon. The last fortnight I seem to have been in bib and tucker from dawn till dusk, listening intently, or pretending to listen intently, to some barmy foreigner droning on about interest rates or the Gulf war, having to drink almost as much in public as I normally do in private and never getting to bed much before four in the morning. All, as far as I could see, in aid of the scheme to rejuvenate poor old Hopalong sufficiently to wheel him in to the White House for another four years.

To this end the Irish Tourist Board agreed to a million dollar ramp based on some fairly fraudulent 'research' by the Let Us Find You An Ancestor Service which is all the rage with the Yanks. Anyway they managed to dig up some half-pissed late Victorian turf-cutter whose signature in the parish register if held upside down might possibly be interpreted as Ryan. This was good enough for the White House, and the PR Circus, complete with ground to air guided missiles, descended on the unsuspecting inhabitants of Ballypoteen (pop. 29), a malodorous hamlet fifty miles from nowhere. The wretched Hopalong was then guided through a charade of lifting Guinness glasses, being given the freedom of the parish, reading out a lot of Bear-baiting rubbish to the alcoholics in the Doil, while Nancy, togged out as Miss Aer Lingus 1931, was wound up to perform a brief walkabout for the reptiles beside the green waters of the Liffey.

By the time we took delivery of them, O'Darby and O'Joan were therefore in a very dazed state, not certain what country they were in and pretty short on the small talk. I knew it was going to be hell the moment I saw them tottering down the aircraft steps hand in hand. The Boss very gallantly went into a clinch with the old gun-slinger for the benefit of the reptiles, and even I had to accept a bird-like peck from the emaciated spousette who clearly thought I was the Duke of Edinburgh. (I may say that after being mauled by the Dallas Giants during Mark's recent courting rituals I am used to this sort of thing.) I had even boned up on the kind of drinks they like and Boris and I concocted a knockout cocktail containing Bourbon and Drinking Chocolate with a cherry in it, which I felt sure would shut them up for the rest of the evening. Alas I had reckoned without the four regiments of heavily armed security men who came along for the ride, one of whom sniffed at my offering and ordered it all to be poured down the sink.

I had been hoping, as you know, to join the Major and his Royal Corps of Winos for the Normandy Anniversary outing, and I am told I missed a bender never to be forgotten. Apparently the old boy was so plastered by the time the march past came that he called the Eyes Right when the Queen was on the other side. But the Duke had had a few himself and it all passed off in gales of laughter. M., however, suspecting that she might be knocked into the B Team by Heads of State like Grand Duke Charlie of Luxemburg, had cried off, so I was forbidden to go on the charabanc.

Before you could say knife however Hoppo was back, this time for the damnfool Economic Summit, which involved cordoning off the whole of London, dragging the Serpentine, and the general buggering up of life as we know it. You might wonder what conceivable point there could be in laying on this Madame

'. . . might possibly be interpreted as Ryan . . .'

Tussaud's jamboree with all these famous faces crammed round a table having their photographs taken, reading out scripts they couldn't understand and listening to same for hours on end, little Howe shuffling about in the background trying to look purposeful. The answer is that, once again, it's all going to look good in Newsweek – the Court of Good King Ron with attendant Lickspittles, Vassals and Serfs Paying Homage. In fact, as you may have gathered, they gave the old boy a pretty rough ride on interest rates, the Boss's voice waxing particularly shrill on this topic and Trousseau wearing a CND badge jumping up and down like a demented fairy. All to no effect, needless to say, as Hopalong by this time had sunk into a coma, still muttering 'Glad to have you know me' and 'Have a nice day'.

Far from having any effect, indeed, Furniss at the NatWest tells me that they've only been waiting for the caravan to leave town before bunging interest rates over here up another couple of notches, which is good news for Wise Virgins like you and me whatever the Boss may say.

The Smellysocks got very excited last week when they discovered a letter from one of M's lackeys in Whitehall ordering the mass bribery of the Railwaymen to stop them backing Brother Scargill. This was supposed to prove that the Boss was secretly in charge of the whole operation. Would that she were! As far as I can see all she does is take calls from the wizened guru of the Kalahari, Laurens van der Pump, who tells her that Mars is moving into her cusp and she must fulfil her destiny. All very well, but where does it leave the rest of us? I enclose some brochures from the bucket shop, offering cheapos to SA where Mr Botha said we'd be welcome to spend a few days any time we like at his Safari Centre above Jo'burg. Sounds like port and lemon time to me, but I suppose we could engage a party of the locals to porter up a few crates together with our clubs. Give us a bell should the spirit move you.

Yours pro tem,

DENIS

10 Downing Street
Whitehall

Dear Bill,

You say that everyone in the Club is speculating like billy-o about
the identity of the Cabinet Minister supposedly caught with his
bags down in the company of a miner during the last election.
Boris and I have carried out what research we could and I will tell
you our findings when we meet on Thursday. The point is that I
have been warned by someone I am unable to name, to wit a
certain person of the female gender who must be obeyed, that if I
put anything in writing whatsoever I will be deemed to have
committed a criminal libel and be left to rot away my few remaining days in the Tower of London. Of course I know who it is, and
between the two of us I wasn't a bit surprised, as I have always
had my doubts about this particular individual and have never
scrupled to say so loud and clear. Anyway you can tell the Major
that if he's putting money on Hailsham in the Club Sweepstake
he may as well kiss it goodbye.

Meanwhile the great battle against King Arthur and his
Squareheads rages unabated with no sign of a let-up at this end.
You should have been with me at the RAC when they showed
Scargill on the news 'falling over' during the Battle of Orgreave.
Cheers? There wasn't a piece of furniture left intact. Windows
broken, toupees thrown in the air – that old retired Brigadier in
the wheelchair who hadn't spoken since the Coronation actually
rose to his feet, threw his crutches away, had a heart attack and
died. A good way to go was what we all said afterwards.

Back at HQ however they were less jubilant. MacGregor's
latest wheeze was to send out a billet doux at phenomenal
expense in postal charges to every miner in the country, telling
him that his intentions have been honourable throughout, and
that things have been hideously twisted by Brother S. for his own
political ends, the hope being that the sooty-faced sons of toil will
blub their eyes out on reading it and 'drift back to work'. Fat lot
of good this will achieve if they are stopped in mid-drift by hordes
of bottle-throwing yobbos bussed in by Wedgwood Benn.

The only solution in my view, as I told MacGregor the last time
I caught him shuffling in through the tradesmen's entrance for

'. . . a Mafia Style gathering at Number Ten . . .'

his daily conflab with the Boss, is to bring in the army and give
them a whiff of grapeshot. Some hope however of any such
robust solution with M. and her cringeing band of paedophiles at
the helm, trying to keep their spirits up with reading aloud
manifestly forged letters from starving miners' wives pledging
their support. They haven't even the guts to implement the new
laws brought in by Tebbit although how the Boys in Blue are
supposed to arrest the entire staff of British Rail and seize their

Art Collection I agree is not altogether clear at this moment in time.

Did you hear my friend Princess Margaret on the wireless being in The Archers? I thought she did jolly well. Her voice sounded completely clear and the way she said 'Good Evening' moved both Boris and me to tears. Our own efforts for the NSPCC were a good deal more lugubrious, involving as they did a Mafia-style gathering at Number Ten attended by various padded-shouldered international hoodlums and share sharks who had paid up to five hundred grand a plate in their search for respectability. M's lot got the idea from Barbara Cartland and her moneygrubbing daughter who lure the Yankee Tourists into their crumbling pile on roughly the same basis. The 'guest of honour' was a retired Kamikaze pilot called Mr Phuwatascorcha, well over ninety and without a word of English. Apparently he subsequently asked for some of his money back on the grounds that I went to sleep while he was telling me via his interpreter of the advances made by the Japanese in disposable softwear. (You will remember in Maurice's case it turned out to be not so disposable as he hoped.) Obviously I wasn't asleep, and had merely closed my eyes in order to concentrate better on what the little Johnny was saying. But the reptiles got hold of it and I was back on the mat yet again at sparrowfart the next morning, threatened with compulsory drying out at that place Maurice goes to near Dorking.

I am still trying to get out of another Swiss Misery Tour at Chateau Despair. I gather the widow Glover is feeling fairly pissed off with M. descending year after year and treating the place like a hotel, but I don't imagine that will deter Margaret.

Yrs in extremis,

DENIS

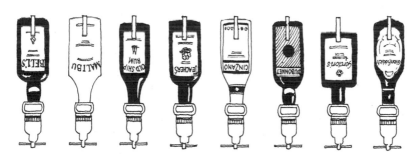

Dear Bill,

I'm afraid our little outing to Sandwich ended in disaster. Maurice has never been good in hot weather and with the temperature pushing ninety quite healthy people were keeling over like ninepins. That was in the bar. God knows what was happening outside on the fairway. According to one of the Battle of Britain boys, Maurice took one of the heavier trophies into the gents under his coat and by the time they'd brought him under control he'd done an estimated five thousand pounds' worth of damage to the vitreous enamel. They were going to call in the police but I pulled rank on the blower from Number Ten late that night and they've agreed to waive charges on condition that the sum is found by the end of the month and that we never bring him there again. A pity, as the old boy lives just down the road. I suppose there's always Littlestone and with so many weirdos down there, Maurice will seem like a pillar of respectability.

When I got back there was a message to call Furniss, asking me whether I would look in on the way to the Club next morning. It seems, as I predicted at the time of that barmy economic summit in aid of Hopalong's re-election campaign, that Wall Street has failed to respond to the massed European pleas for a dip in interest rates, with the result that the pound is rapidly going through the floor and the NatWest is jacking up its base rates with immediate effect. With this in mind, Furniss was hoping that I would see the advantages of their Golden Wonder Added Interest Deposit Account with the Three Day Withdrawal Facility. I took half a bottle of his disgusting sherry off him and said I would mull it over but between you and me I think the only hope is to shift the caboodles over to the US pdq. The Boy Mark is in situ and miserable little viper though he may be, I think he can be trusted to cross the road to the Chase Manhattan and fill in a couple of pink forms.

This cold wind from America seems to have concentrated M's mind on the Scargill Scenario and by the time I got back after lunch MacGregor had been whistled in. I bumped into him shortly after six coming in through the back door for an

'. . . drafted in to do my Old Heathers act . . .'

emergency pow-wow with the Boss and Walker, and it being Boris's day off I was drafted in to do my Old Heathers act with the amber fluid. Margaret kicked off by saying yet again that the Miners' Strike was no business of hers, Walker sitting there nodding, and that she had no wish at all to interfere. This seemed pretty damn silly to me and MacGregor obviously thought the same, but the old boy knows when to keep his trap shut. The Boss then embarked on a long lecture about the economics of energy and how she couldn't understand what all the trouble was about. At this the old codger stirred feebly in his chair, wheezed heavily, and seemed to go a little wild about the eyes. 'But surely, but surely, I understood . . .' he began, 'I understood that it was your intention to squeeze Scargill until his eyes popped out. Wasn't that what you said?'

I could have told him from my long years under the Iron Heel that the presentation of hostile evidence never goes down very well and Margaret's eyes took on a steelier glint. 'Memory can play strange tricks, Mr MacGregor,' she snapped, 'particularly if people let themselves go . . .' Here a glance at Old Heathers tactfully replenishing his own tumbler set the socks a-smouldering. 'You know quite well that I have scrupulously avoided becoming involved in your undignified blood feud with the National Union of Mineworkers. Peter and I have always urged you to seek a compromise that was satisfactory to both sides . . .' The one-time City Nabob here made a cautious gesture with one hand: 'I think the Prime Minister means that we would have so urged, ahem, had we ever, at any time, been in touch with you, which of course we were not.'

I could see poor Mr MacG. twitching a bit at this, so I lunged forward with the silver tray to top up his trembling beaker. Shortly after that I was told to hop it, but the old boy was in there for a good solid hour before he tottered out looking white and shaken and was helped into his Roller. I was not surprised when Boris told me the next morning that secret talks between MacG. and Scargill were going on in a guest house in Moscow Road, Bayswater.

Did you see that Nigerian Airways are running a new one-way 'Chief Dikkoo' cheapo? Free dope before take-off, own tasteful stripped pine stateroom with personal air-conditioning and no charge whatsoever. Sounds to me as though they ought to introduce it on the Falklands Run.

Talking of dopey diplomats you probably saw that Mogadon man was shipped in and out of Moscow. In my opinion they'd have been much wiser to leave him there.

The Widow Glover has been persuaded to let down her drawbridge yet again so your Mexican Tequila Package will have to wait. In the interim, I look forward to our little outing to the Algarve. See you at Gatwick 9.30 sharp in time for a pre-flight stiffener.

Yrs awash,

DENIS

Dear Bill,

Goodness me, what a beano! The bill for breakages arrived from the Portuguese Embassy the morning after I got back, but I am pleading diplomatic immunity. I formed the impression that we may have been forgiven by Mother Flack herself, as she was fully insured and the thatched beach hut was never very solidly built, as you will remember from the time when Maurice did his gorilla from the crossbeam and had to be taken to the local Out-patients. Those ex-pats have always been too full of beans in my view and fooling about with fireworks last thing at night is always asking for trouble. The locals' equivalent to the National Trust claimed five miles of coastal woodland destroyed but I'm sure they were exaggerating.

The Boss hasn't come down since her big end-of-term jamboree at Halitosis Hall. Kinnock and his chums decided that they would go out with a bang, Vote of No Confidence, all the big guns wheeled in, Boss to be brought to her knees and have her nose rubbed in it, forced to confess country ruined, she herself hopeless incompetent, Cabinet a crew of bungling eighth-raters. You'd think under the circs they could have made some of it stick, but it is beginning to dawn on these thick-headed proles that Brother Kinnock, amiable enough over half a pint of shandy in the Varsity Bar, is just not of the stature to go ten rounds with Meaty Margaret the Iron Mauler.

The poor little bugger is in any case a martyr to chronic laryngitis, brought on, as with many of his compatriots, by verbal diarrhoea. (You remember Taffy Patterson in the REME who used to empty the mess at Catterick with his reminiscences of life in the Valleys. He always had a packet of Meggozones to hand to lubricate his wheezing chords.) Anyway poor little Pillock got to his feet to administer the coup de grace – French, as the Major's Mother always used to say, for lawnmover – croaked a few defiant scraps of Welsh rhetoric barely audible above the usual undertow of flatulence and Trotskyite heckling, whereupon the Mauler rose, twisted his neck in a reef-knot and began whirling him

'. . . *Maurice did his Gorilla from the crossbeam . . .*'

round and round her head much to the delight of her young cohorts. Lawson unfortunately then managed to put his foot in it when he said that the Coal Strike was good news for the City, then said he hadn't said it, and Tebbit had to get up and say he had said it and it was a jolly good thing too. The Boss was spitting tintacks at this as it was meant to be her Big Night and she didn't want Nicely Nicely and Mr Munster giving the gallery anything to get their teeth into.

Not that it makes much difference as the Old Girl is now so carried away with her Thousand Year Reich that she has declared a Polish-style amnesty for all the old wrecks on the scrap heap and is even talking of bringing back smarmy-boots Parkinson, the evil lothario of yesteryear. A great mistake in my view. Once a chap has been caught with his trousers down behind the pav the chances are it'll happen again, Ethiop can't change his spots etc. As I said to Picarda in the Executive Jet on the way back from the Algarve, how do we know he hasn't got love-children everywhere like Prosser-Cluff, who had them in Singapore every colours of the rainbow. Of course out there it didn't matter.

Mind you the Cabinet is getting a bit like the England Cricket Team and the way things are going she may have to take any old tramp off the Embankment. Fatty P., as you probably saw, is taking voluntary redundancy after five hard years in Siberia, the Monk looks to me pretty near the edge most of the time, little Jenkin (P.) is unanimously deemed to be ripe for the knacker's yard, and poor old Hailsham will have to give himself up to the men in white coats one of these days before they come in and get him. I can't for the life of me remember what the other ones' names are.

Howe, admittedly, seems to be gathering laurels from every side, though why I haven't got a blind idea. They all trooped off to the Land of the Yellow Peril and got a piece of paper from Mr Dung on the Hong Kong question saying he would allow the old China Heads, Opium Pedlars and other rickshaw fodder to live on in the manner to which they have become accustomed for another five hundred years after the lease runs out. But why anyone should believe a word those slit-eyed little fiends have to say I can't imagine. You and I have had dealings with Johnny Chink and know that all he understands is the big stick wielded by White Sahib with gusto and without pity. Howe, who has spent all his life pushing peas round his plate in the lawcourts canteen, doesn't begin to grasp these subtleties. Give him a beaker of fermented beanshoots Number Fifty Three and he's anybody's, to say nothing of his Foreign Office advisers. Nuff said.

You may have seen in the Court Circular that the Widow Glover, bless her elasticated stockings, has once again deigned to play host to the Old Codgers for a limited season. I've been trying to find out if that ghastly shrink who was there last year is going to be in attendance but the Widow plays her cards very close to her chest and all she vouchsafed over the phone to M. was that she was very taken with spiritualism and the F-Plan Diet and had either of us ever attended a seance? Margaret persists in the economic argument, i.e. five-star luxury, no reptiles, no bill. But every time I think of it my heart contracts with terror. No postcards from Ibiza please, I couldn't bear it.

Yours in a trance,

DENIS

SCHLOSS BANGELSTEIN
BIRCHERMUESLI
SWITZERLAND 24 AUGUST 1984

Dear Bill,

If I told you that I spent seven hours last night sitting in a padded box costing £4,500 for the evening listening to assorted members of the Master Race warbling away ad nauseam in incomprehensible Italian in a theatre crammed to the ceiling with overweight music lovers all of whom looked like Maurice Picarda's grandmother, you will understand why the Queen Mother's hipflask gusset has been doing sterling service since our arrival here.

You may remember from last year that the Widow G., proprietor of this Alpine Morgue and inheritor of a vast collection of daubs all authenticated by the late Sir Anthony Blunt, has a warm rapport with a certain Herr Bosendorfer, a bearded trick-cyclist and close personal friend of Van der Pump. His new passion, shared by the Widow, is for what he calls 'ze divine Mozart', who, it transpires, was resident in an adjacent watering hole where he worked for many years as a bandleader before coming to a sticky end from over-indulgence. When the Boss and I checked in at the beginning of the week, we therefore found that we were booked on a season ticket for the next three nights to listen to the Maestro's oeuvre at what was described as 'nearby Salzburg'.

On with the bib and tucker, crammed into the back of Herr Hanfstaengel's obsolete hearse, Bosendorfer reeking of Old Swiss Rocky Mountain Shag and bubbling through his meerschaum in a most disgusting manner and off down the hairpin descent. Three hours later, green at the gills, we are deposited by the smirking little bugger at the wheel outside the Festspielhaus to be greeted with a barrage of Kraut flashbulbs and the oleaginous Master of Ceremonies one Hubert von Caravan, soon slobbering over Margaret's paw and babbling away about the honour she has bestowed on their 'leedel Fest'.

Hanfstaengel, I realised, had every reason to grin as he was going to spend the evening with his companions in the Golden Horn, beyond whose welcoming doors I could see a number of obese burghers in leather shorts all getting stuck into the flaming brandy and stone jugs of Heineken. Von Caravan caught me gazing wistfully in this direction, slapped me powerfully on the back with a sadistic leer and said 'Come on, Herr Thatcher, only five hours to go to the first interval.'

The pong of aftershave and fancy French scent almost swamped that of Bosendorfer's pipe. No air conditioning and too dark in the box even to read the newspaper. There was a bit of the usual scraping and sawing from the M.U. down below decks, then absolute silence. Von Caravan, it emerged, is a very bumptious bugger and had trodden on the toes of the local Scargill, prompting a down tools on the orchestra floor. The curtain finally went up at about nine o'clock, by which time my throat was like the Sahara and I was in no mood to appreciate why the Count had dressed up as a woman and jumped out of the window into the arms of the gardener, also for some reason dressed as a woman and singing in a high soprano voice. I may have got this slightly wrong, because shortly afterwards I drifted off into a profound sleep and dreamed that you and I and Maurice were playing golf on an ocean liner with Edmundo Ros conducting a choir of trained seals in the saloon.

Bosendorfer, to whom I confided this experience in the interval, said the sea always betokened sexual frustration and the symbolism of the golf clubs should be pretty obvious, even to me.

'. . . I drifted off into a profound sleep . . .'

Dirty Bugger. During the second half and on subsequent evenings I succeeded in hammering myself into insensibility with miniature stickies smuggled in at a price by Hanfstaengel. I find that if I wear a very stiff shirt it stops me from keeling over.

Back at the Schloss we discovered that the Widow G's initial enquiries about spiritualism were no mere ploy to put us off. On the first non-musical evening, hoping for an early night, I was slinking away from the table only to be beckoned back. Menials having cleared away the biscuit crumbs and bubbles of mineral water, a stout, swarthy woman with a bristling moustache called Frau Balogh who had kept pretty quiet during dinner closed her eyes and asked us all to place our hands palms down on the table, our little fingers touching. She then enquired in a foghorn voice whether anybody was there. There was silence for a time. Then the old bird began making burbling noises and asked if one of us had a friend called Stebbings. Quite frankly, Bill, I never thought there was anything in this sort of caper and you could have knocked me down with a bargepole. Before I could own up, Reggie's voice came through clear as a bell, sounding as though he'd had a few, and describing his life 'over there'. 'We're all very, very, very happy', he said with a bit of a German accent. 'Jolly decent crowd in the Club House and I'm now living with a nice Red Indian woman. Give my best to Maurice and the Major and let me know when you're coming so I can bag you a place at the bar. It doesn't sound very jolly where you are.' Luckily the old boy signed off at this point or it might have got rather embarrassing. The next caller was Mozart, speaking with an even thicker German accent, thanking us for motoring all that way, and did anyone have a bit of manuscript paper as he had a new waltz he wanted to dictate. The old bird then burst into song, but it sounded to me very like the Blue Danube.

Talking of people going into a trance, I saw in the Airmail Edition of the Daily Telegraph (25 Swiss Francs) that poor old Hopalong has taken to nodding off during his brief spells on duty and that Nancy now has to be on hand to answer his questions for him. But he's clearly not like that all the time and I thought his plan for bombing Russia was very sound and proves that at that moment at least he was absolutely on the ball. I wonder if the Boss will soldier on into her dotage. I shall certainly be elsewhere by then, whooping it up with Stebbings and Co. in some far-off pavilion, so she'll have to rely on the Boy Gummer to blow into her ear trumpet.

Must toddle down to the Edelweiss Tea Rooms to 'catch the post' (code for a bottle and a half of the gentian-flavoured fire-water at Herr Davis's Pull-Up for Goatherds.)

Yours till the shadows fall,

DENIS

10 Downing Street
Whitehall

Dear Bill,

Hope you got my p.c. frae Bonnie Deeside. An unusually dreary episode this year, even by the standards of Castle O'Doom. The D of E had invited some miserable little Japanese Johnny called Prince Fujiama in the hopes of winning the hissing Nip round to support his Ban the Whale Campaign. Quite frankly I'm beginning to think our Greek friend, though a doughty sniffer of the cork and teller of ribald yarns over the stickies and cigars, is just a gnat's out of touch with the modern world, and I speak as one against whom the same accusation has from time to time been brought by certain pushier members of the Club.

Margaret, who now seems to have the Queen very well trained, had led the ladies off to watch a re-run of The Two Ronnies in the Highland Lounge, leaving me, the Nip and His Grace to toy with the tiny thistle-shaped sticky-thimbles. 'One thing I wanted to ask you, Thatcher,' said the D of E, 'what's this thing called Income Tax? You don't have it down your way, do you, Hiro?' The Japanese bird, somewhat the worse for wear after a couple of hours with the Queen Mum, picked a piece of shot out of his oversize dentures, inclined his head and said 'Ah So' a couple of times in the way that they do, leaving it to me to enlighten old Rip Van Battenberg on how us working class folk had to hand over every brass farthing we earn to Lawson and Co. to give away to layabouts, drones, scrimshankers and striking miners. I may say it crossed my mind to add that a hefty slice of the hard-earned caboodle was siphoned off to keep His Nibs and numerous family in the style to which they had become accustomed, but discretion intervened. I discover since I got back that the economics lesson I had unfolded was regurgitated word for word by HRH in that magazine they give away free on aeroplanes.

Strictly entre nous I think poor old MacGregor's finally blown a gasket. You probably saw the photograph of him running round with a plastic bag over his head pretending to be a chicken. Friends said afterwards he was in fact about to be sick at the thought of another confrontation with King A. the Kremlin's friend, which is very understandable, but anyway the talking

'. . . leaving me, the Nip, and his Grace . . .'

shop appears pro tem to have been closed down once again. M. is pretty pleased at the way things are going. I think she has always had this vision of a forty-eight round contest to the death in the square ring and at the end of it the once-proud King Arthur, battered and bleeding, being led in chains from the arena with his gumshield knocked down his throat. The wets, including Dead

Eye Whitelaw who always whimper at the sight of blood, have been pleading for the referee to go in and stop the fight. However Mr Munster (Tebbit N.) is urging her to go on till the final bell, by which time they hope there won't be any pits left to close down and everything will be hunkydory.

Poor old Fatty Prior, the while, has wisely taken his copper handshake and buggered off to the boardroom, for which I cannot say I blame him. He is to be replaced by the stuck-up ex-FO greaser Hurd, who has about as much chance of bringing peace to the war-torn province as Danny la Rue. He is to be hindered in these endeavours by Muttonchops Boyson, who between ourselves has been hitting the optics pretty heavily of late. The other new recruit to the Cabinet is a friend of Maurice Picarda's called Young who used to be in property and has spent the last few years shimmering about Finchley making a bob or two out of various big deals. His task is to foster the illusion that Margaret is worried sick about unemployment and has numerous schemes up her sleeve to create jobs and scupper the opposition's little tricks on that front.

Did you see that uppity quack Owen has been sounding off about the Belgrano? My advice was to come clean and say what the hell is war about if it's not torpedoeing a boatload of Argies before they steam in and do the same to us, but for the Boss this is a very sore point, her finest hour etc, and any word of criticism brings on the heebie-jeebies. In this I think she was encouraged by Tarzan, and they have now decided to string up some little Whitehall paper-pusher called Ponting, rack, thumbscrews, the whole works, just because he photostated a few memos and sent them down to Halitosis Hall.

Must go now. That little runt Gordon Reece has blown in to put us through our paces for the Conference. The Boss, as I understand it, is to appear in battleship grey with steel handbag and accessories to suggest a resolute Autumn Mood, with myself in beige to strike a note of mellow optimism. We get the words later. If I can lay down smoke and beetle over to Pyecombe we might manage a few rounds and I can assure you that Deadeye will not be asked this year. God knows what he might do with a niblick after lunch.

T.T.F.N.

Yours aye,

DENIS

10 Downing Street
Whitehall

5 OCTOBER 1984

Dear Bill,

The more I think about it, the more I regret my weakness in not
insisting on Archie Wellbeloved being given the Canterbury job.
Admittedly, as I may have said before, the poor old sod had one
foot in the grave (as opposed to the present score of two), and his
sermons had become pretty weird to put it mildly, but no power
on earth would have persuaded him to allow a rabid revolutionary
like Bishop Jenkins to occupy any senior position in the firm.
Runcie in my opinion is a walking disaster, utterly spineless,
in very much the same mould as that padre we had at Aldershot
who tried to have the Clap Parade held behind closed doors on
compassionate grounds.

As you may recall the Boss had to carpet the silly bugger after
his boshed Thanksgiving Service for the Falklands which he
turned into some kind of pacifist rally. Unrepentant, the daft old
sod appoints this dreadful god-botherer to Durham, despite the
fact that Comrade J. has made it clear he thinks the whole bang
shoot is a lot of rubbish. I myself as you know am not a deeply
religious person, though I've always believed in turning up for
church parade, but I must confess when the bolt of lightning
struck the Minster the morning after he'd been wheeled in, it did
give one pause for thought. Bishop Trotkins however failed to get
the message and the first thing he did on climbing into the pulpit
was to trumpet away at the top of his voice to the effect that
MacGregor was past it and should be shipped back pdq to the US
of A. All of which may be perfectly sound over the stickies and
cigars and indeed coincides with my own opinion, but it is not the
sort of thing a senior sky-pilot is employed to say when dressed
up in his full rig with the cameras turning and the grubby reptiles
squatting under the pulpit, pencils poised, waiting to seize on
anything remotely controversial.

As you can imagine, the Boss blew her top in no uncertain
manner. She may not be a very religious person either but she is
firmly convinced, quite rightly, that the Almighty is one of us,
and that Old Nick lines up with Arthur Scargill and his Moscow
minions. I made the mistake of toddling in with the clubs just

31

after she'd seen Trotkins' outburst on the news and got it full in the neck.

Wasn't there a King in the history books who was always getting stick from some rabble-rousing saint or other and in the end dropped a hint to a couple of his heavies that he wouldn't be all that depressed if the aforementioned Red Cleric was rubbed out? On this occasion it turned out that I myself came within a whisker of having to get in the motor, drive up the M1 and pump lead into the troublesome bish. Eventually, however, wiser counsels prevailed and M. snatched up the blower to give an earful to Runcie. Pretty good stuff, entre nous, and I had refilled my glass no less than four times before she replaced the receiver. The gist of it was that if it hadn't been for her he would still be ladling out the swill on the pig-farm down in St Albans, an object of ridicule and contempt. As it was he was now an international star, allowed to dress up in silly frocks for the delight of millions of viewers all over the world. Point Two, MacGregor was her oldest and closest friend, very prone to depression and already under considerable strain, and remarks of the kind made by Runcie's Red appointee could very well cause him intense personal distress.

Cantuar I don't think managed to get a word in though I could hear him bleating faintly at the other end whenever Margaret paused for breath. Anyway, upshot was that he was to bike a letter round to old Mr McGoo personally apologising, and then get on to Trotkins and boot his spine through the top of his mitre. M. then telephoned Sir D. English, smarmy little creep, and told him to clear the front page of the Daily Mail for the shock exclusive that Runcie was on his knees praying for forgiveness.

The moment he spies the paper the next morning, of course, Runcie being Runcie and having no sense of dignity, goes on the wireless and says he hasn't apologised at all, Jenkins a damn good bloke, quite right to sound off, a shepherd responsible for giving voice on behalf of his sheep, which only drove the Boss into further paroxysms.

Unwelcome returnee of the week, bouncing in on his brothel creepers and clearly the worse for wear, was our former neighbour Mogadon Man, cock a hoop at his big deal with Brother Chink. The gist of it is, as far as I could tell, that Honkers falls to the Yellow Peril after a suitable interval, during which our fat cats will have time to remove their funds to somewhere safe in the Cayman Islands. I may have said this before but the trouble with

'. . . to give an earful to Runcie . . .'

these lawyers like Howe is that they never got their knees brown out East as you and I did. The most inexperienced China hand knows only too well that Saving Face is the name of the game, and that Johnny Chinaman will always tell you exactly what you want to hear. Howe however got pretty shirty when I suggested that the Chinese might choose to ignore the small print while M. herself told me that I had no knowledge of diplomacy and that the Chinese were men of their word. It crossed my mind to enquire what the word was but by then they were toasting each other in the Mogadon's duty-free Rice Whisky and the latter was holding forth, poor short-arsed little sod, about his plans for single-handedly bringing about a thaw in East-West relations.

My plans for Brighton are as follows: Check in Hotel Metropole Tuesday a.m. Photo-call to establish presence. Mid-morning unexpected Telemessage arrives announcing Emergency Board Meeting Picwarmth Ltd. Arrive Pyecombe 12.15 view copious snorts with yourself, Maurice and the Major. Hideyhole chez Maurice's aunt Freda, Pyecombe 312, ask for 'Mr Simpson'.

Yrs unquenchably,

DENIS

 10 Downing Street
Whitehall

19 OCTOBER 1984

Dear Bill,
Very decent of you to ring following the Brighton bomb blast. Your concern much appreciated. I'm afraid I can tell you very little about the 'incident' itself as I had retired to bed following a pretty heavy fringe meeting of the Conservative Friends of Grape and Grain (F.O.G.G.), at which I had done perhaps a little too much research into the second category. Hardly had my head touched the pillow than I was plunged into a dreamless state of oblivion, from which I was only woken by the Night Porter telling me that the Grand had collapsed during the night, and would I make my way quietly down the fire escape.

The Boss, needless to say, took the whole thing very much in her stride, rather like that Campbell woman who was catapulted out of Bluebird at a hundred and fifty m.p.h. After a few comforting words to the Boys in Blue, she resumed the preparation of her speech to Conference. I myself tottered down to the TV lounge, where a jolly Red Cross lady was ladling out medicinal snorts to those suffering from shock.

Oddly enough the whole thing seemed to have rather an

'. . . a jolly Red Cross lady was ladling out medicinal snorts . . .'

encouraging effect on the general morale, until then the moaning minnies having had the best of the argument. Bloody Runcie started it all. The sheep-featured primate himself claimed that it was all fixed by the press, he had no idea the Conference was coming up etc. etc., but there he was across half a page of *The Times* on the opening day, just like Parkinson the year before, bleating away about the unacceptable face of the Boss and the need for everyone to come together in a spirit of woolly benevolence. Usual Guardian rubbish, time for Scargill and McGoo to kiss and make up etc.

The effect of this was to put new spine into the wets who all promptly came popping out of the woodwork berating the Proprietor for her lack of compassion. I don't usually have much time for Mr Munster but I thought he was very sound, particularly on TV, in putting Runcie in his place. In case you missed it, the point he made was that the chap in the Bible who lent a helping hand to the poor old Samaritan or whoever it was who got mugged, wouldn't have been able to get him into intensive care at a local hotel had it not been for the fact that he was a businessman of enterprise and initiative with a pretty healthy credit balance at the NatWest of the day. A very good point, I thought, that Runcie might well put in his pipe and ponder before he next sounds off.

Just before the bomb put an end to the bickering, Walker threw his toupee into the ring with a few scarcely veiled cracks at M., egged on no doubt by the usual seedy gang of Yesterday's Men, e.g. Cemetery Face Gilmour, gloomy little Pym and poor old Sailor Ted. However all these things were forgotten in the Warrior Queen Reborn scenario: show must go on, men of violence whether in the bogs or down the mines to be resisted to the last breath, law and order to be upheld, Old Bill given pat on back, but delegates never to forget that M. deeply concerned about the plight of the unemployed etc. far so more than any woolly-haired cleric or whingeing wet like Walker. All of which may or may not be true, though in my experience compassion has never come all that high on the Boss's list of Top Ten Virtues. As for Lawson, if you ask me he is about as compassionate as a traffic warden with a hangover.

We've had the odd chuckle watching poor old Hopalong getting the bird for his TV debate with Mondale. My own view is that he was perfectly all right so long as he had his prompter screen with all his words written out in capital letters and the sincere bits underlined, but that it was tantamount to insanity to let him go on without his apparatus. At Burmah he'd have got his golden handshake years ago. Why they can't introduce compulsory retirement for politicos the same as anyone else I cannot understand. You've only got to look at Hailsham gazing round and trying to remember where he is to realise the folly of letting these old boys hang on. I saw some wag suggesting that Hopalong should submit to a senility test which consisted of starting at a hundred and counting backwards in sevens. Some of us tried it in the bar the other night and only Prothero got down past eighty before he had a brainstorm and frothed at the mouth. Which only goes to show.

Are you coming to Maurice's birthday party at the Bay Tree?

Yours in one piece,

DENIS

 10 Downing Street
Whitehall
2 NOVEMBER 1984

Dear Bill,

Sorry I couldn't meet up with you and the Major at the Intrepid Stoat but, as you may have gathered from the media, the Chief Frog was in town and we were obliged to hop attendance in an official capacity. I have never trusted the bugger – even though he had quite a decent war and blew up several Boche goods-trains while in the Maquis. Altogether too attentive to the Boss in my view, effusive hand-kissing rituals, Gallic murmurings in the car, bouquets of expensive blooms for ever thrust under the nose, and all the time the wily little eyes clocking up the Eurodollars and plotting means of defrauding our simple-minded farmers of their meagre profits. The Queen Mum had the right attitude in my book: took one look at him and hopped it to Venice in the Royal Yacht with a goodly supply of G & T stashed away below decks.

The rest of us were press-ganged into the Palace of Westminster to listen to the over-inflated Monsieur Grenouille holding forth for half an hour in his native tongue without subtitles. What the hell he was talking about only Hailsham appeared to understand. It fell to him, as he apparently got an 'O' Level French, or the equivalent in the 1890s when he was at Eton, to totter to his feet at the bitter end, weighed down with his moth-eaten robes and other paraphernalia, to propose the vote of thanks. I managed to catch 'Vive la France' and 'Ooh la la', but even Mitterand seemed pretty mystified and looked down his nose in the way they all do when a chap tries to grapple with their absurd lingo.

All was going merry as a funeral bell when – Zut Alors – Inspector Clouseau the comic gendarme en suite decided to test the skills of the Boys in Blue by planting a cache of dynamite under the rhododendron bush in the Embassy Garden and then inviting the Sniffer Division in to hunt the thimble. By some miracle the dogs found the dynamite, but Scotland Yard singularly failed to see the joke after what happened at Brighton and took it as a reflection on their international position. Entre nous J. Frog may well have a point here, as Maurice rang up the other night for a jaw and told me that on the second day of the Conference he and 'a friend' – I presume his Antique Hypermarket Lady – had got stuck in a revolving door at the Grand carrying a load of early firearms for the Fittleworth Antiques Fayre, and when they were extricated booked in for the afternoon under the name of Mr and Mrs Paddy O'Trotsky. Maurice said they were escorted upstairs to the Bridal Suite without anyone batting an eyelid.

Brother Scargill as you see has taken a poke in the eye from the Nacods, whoever they are, closely followed by a pretty good root up the arse from the beak, who ordered him to hand over all his assets to the bailiff. Knowing Scargill I assumed such funds to be already salted away in the Moscow Narodny Bank, but Furniss, with whom I was enjoying the customary Friday morning schooner of Algerian turpentine, explained that in these days of computerised banking it is what he calls 'a whole different ball game'. Once you've got the account number all you do is go to one of these new electronic one-arm bandits, type in a few details, pull the lever and the cash comes shooting out like Niagara. Obviously Arthur hadn't thought of this one and is going to be looking a bit red in the face when it comes to payday for the Formation Brickthrowers who are unlikely to let themselves be fobbed off with a tin of Bulgarian artichokes compliments of Russfam.

Meanwhile on the home front, Walker had also begun to get the wind up and issued instructions to Old Stumblebum McG to keep off the TV and leave the talking to some new man with a Pinko past they had brought in from below stairs who speaks with the right kind of accent and sucks a smelly pipe like Wilson used to. Since then the old boy has been in a sulk and is talking

'. . . stuck in a revolving door at the Grand . . .'

about going back to the States to doze away his few remaining days in the rocking chair on the front porch.

Events in Brighton have continued to pay off very handsomely. M's popularity poll has shot clean through the roof and the Wets have crawled back into their holes. The only fly in the ointment from the Pavilion End is that the whirling-eyed Benn and Old Father Trot Heffer were both blackballed from the Smellysocks Steering Committee, which has rather put the wind up the Saatchis. Benn apparently blotted his copybook by turning up to give out the raffle prizes at the Militant Ball last weekend, which I can only attribute to softening of the brain brought on by excessive tea-drinking.

Trust Maurice to book our Autumn Break in the Balearics with this firm who've just called in the receiver. I smelt a rat when he told me they'd offered him a seat on the Board.

Yrs in the soup,

DENIS

10 Downing Street
Whitehall
16 NOVEMBER 1984

Dear Bill,

Glad to see you for our regular binge after the Cenotaph. I finally found out who the crumpled little bugger with the fifth wreath was, the one we all had such a good chuckle over. Apparently they decided to put Owen's nose out of joint after he'd insisted so much about being allowed in on the act by getting hold of some undertaker bird from Ulster to represent the Orange Extremists. As you could see, security was pretty tight. The Queen Mother was frisked on the way in and even I had to produce means of identification which made me very cross I don't mind telling you. All entirely pointless as it turned out as the IRA's Mrs Big, wanted in connection with five hundred assorted explosions, was that same day tipped off by the police in all the Sunday papers and scarpered for the US of A, home of the brave and land of the free.

Talking of which it's rather amazing, isn't it, about old Hoppo staying in the saddle for another four years? Our American cousins really are a very rum crew. The poor old boy is plainly gaga, a fact which emerged on the one occasion he was allowed out without his prompter. But it's all fixed by a bunch of Hollywood smart-arses with big cigars, and whenever anyone asks a difficult question they let off a lot of balloons and hundreds of chorus girls come in twirling drumsticks, everyone sings 'God bless America' and they all burst into tears.

A far cry I may say from the malodorous Orient whither I was propelled on the sad demise of Mother Gandhi. I never had much time for the old trout myself, but she went down very well with

M. and also, for that matter, with H.M. and as you may remember even starred in the Sandringham Christmas Spectacular last year, which I thought was an error of taste. One could see that despite differences of caste, creed and colour, both the ladies' hearts went out to her for taking a firm line on everything – castrating any males caught wandering about the streets looking randy, clapping her opponents in jail at the drop of a turban – all ideas, I may say, that the Boss has been secretly toying with for some time. Given the excitable nature of her subjects, I agreed with the Major that she had been rather asking for it when she blew up Johnny Sikh's Holy of Holies, as those of us who have been out East could have told her. But with a woman like that there's no point in arguing the toss.

Having had my backside punctured like a colander by the medico at London Airport against swamp fever, beri beri etc., I was in no mood to appreciate the obsequies, especially as I had to share a mini-van in the cavalcade with Steel, Owen and little Kinnock, all of whom had been tucking into the Duty Free and were sweating pretty heavily in their outfits from Tropicadilly Off-the-peg Department. I said to Kinnock, who very generously offered me a swig of his Warrington Vodka, what a good thing it was we didn't do things over here the way they do them over there. Imagine the Boss, which heaven forfend, being set fire to on the Albert Embankment, and then distributed in brass bowls by Red Star throughout the length and breadth of the Kingdom.

Kinnock made the good point too, I thought, that it was a bit ripe the way young Reggie Gandhi stepped into his mother's shoes without so much as a by your leave, and how would I feel if the Boy Mark automatically took up the reins of office in similar circumstances? After this and a few more libations from the domestic vodka I began to take quite a shine to brother Neil and to think that on several other points he was reasonably sound. He told me, entre nous, that he regards Friend Scargill as a prize twat and would be more than ready to crack his skull open with a walking stick should the opportunity present itself. Obviously he's not allowed to say that in public, otherwise he might get the walking stick treatment himself from the hooligan pickets.

A propos the Trots, Tarzan had to go into bat against some pretty tough bodyline stuff when Captain Bob Maxwell, fresh from his escape from the hungry Ethiopian hordes, revealed in his Moscow Gazette that the Min. of Def. had conveniently 'lost'

'. . . an old seadog I found myself next to . . .'

the logbook of the sub that sank the Belgrano, the implication being that it was pretty hot stuff and would otherwise have brought down the government. However what really happened, according to an old seadog I found myself next to at the Cenotaph, was that the helmsman had in fact taken the logbook home to impress his grandmother and she'd stuffed it in the boiler owing to the coal shortage. What I can't understand is why Heseltine didn't stand up and say that in the House. These people just make life difficult for themselves.

Re your enquiry about whether you should buy into British Telecom. Lawson's so snooty he won't even give me the time of day, but Maurice P. says they're going to be a goldmine so I should draw your own conclusions.

May Shiva's many arms fill your pockets with good things.

DENIS

 10 Downing Street
Whitehall

30 November 1984

Dear Bill,

I don't know whether you ever have the wireless on in the bath? If so you may have heard the very entertaining cabaret last week when the Smellysocks ran amuck at Halitosis Hall, shouted down poor little Fowler, called him an animal, tried to pull his trousers down and stamped on his sandwiches. Heffer, the ring leader, even breathed on his spectacles, so I was told.

The whole thing was got up by Scargill's paid agents in the House, who claimed that M. was ruthlessly robbing the piggy banks of widows and orphans in the Yorkshire Wastes in order to induce their menfolk to join the trickle back to work. I may say if it had been left to me every damn penny would have been docked. Why we should pay out all our directors' salaries and other dividends so that the miners can go on lobbing petrol bombs at the Boys in Blue quite passes my understanding. Margaret agrees, entre nous, but couldn't get it past the Saatchis.

Despite this setback they seem to think it'll be all over by Christmas, and the only real talking point is what to do with the defeated King Arthur. Should he be led in chains through Threadneedle Street or will there be a lot of pie in the sky from the Wets about no one being the winner, now is the time to kiss and make up etc? My own solution, which the Proprietor seems ready to rubber-stamp when the time comes, is for Scargill to be doped, crated up and dispatched on a one-way ticket to Moscow via Aeroflot. Act Two: A full-scale Thanksgiving in St Paul's to be conducted by the snaggle-toothed Archbishop and his Bench of Trots, at gunpoint if necessary.

Since I saw you last at the R.A.C. – and thank you for a slap-up blow-out with all the trimmings (I assume you can swing it on expenses – next one on me) we have been entertaining Fitzgerald the Dublin Teasock, a tall gangling bean very much out of his depth, but like most of his race no mean sniffer of the cork. Despite the rigorous security (every field and hedgerow within miles of Chequers bristling with Panzer Divisions) and the For Your Eyes Only timetable, all the reptiles were on parade at the gates, including those who had just returned from interviewing the World's Most Wanted Woman in her attractive terraced house in Dunleary, who in fact was obviously somebody quite different.

Fitzgerald plainly had no idea what was coming to him. He turned up with a file of suggestions about the way ahead which it took three men to carry and which the Boss proceeded to tear up one by one in front of the television cameras, while that oily little Hurd sniggered obsequiously at her side. You could see from FitzG's eyes that this made him very upset as they'd spent months working on them and after it was over I felt obliged to lay an arm round the poor old boozer and lead him away to the smoking room where we killed off a brace of Jamieson's King Size.

He's actually very sound on most topics, agreed with me that Hurd was a four-letter fellow of the first water and seemed reassured by my own view that we should hand back the whole bang shoot to the natives a.s.a.p. As he pointed out while demonstrating a very amusing penny-throwing game they play over there, the only result of M. getting on her high horse was that his lot would get the heave-ho and she would find herself having to do business with that little shyster Haughey and serve her bloody well right. I think it might have been at the back of his mind that I would share this thought with Margaret in the privacy of the boudoir, but that only goes to show he doesn't know much about how to deal with the Boss.

The only thing that's really got up the old girl's nose of recent days was old Walrusfeatures Macmillan coming back from the grave and attempting with shaking hand to plunge the dagger between her shoulder blades. According to a friend of the Major's who runs a lupin farm near Birch Grove, what brought the old bugger out of the woodwork was Emmanuel Shinwell slipping in

'. . . Walrusfeatures MacMillan coming back from the grave . . .'

to do his soft-shoe number in the Other Place at the age of a hundred. Bovvermac was determined to show that even if he was a mere stripling of ninety he could knock spots off Manny any time and, unlike his competitor, still put the boot in. Picture the scene. Massed ranks of ermined geriatrics weeping quietly into their pocket handkerchiefs. A lot of guff about the old days, First World War, camaraderie of the trenches, and what it all boiled down to was that Margaret was a heartless little woman who was leading us all up the garden path. Fortunately they were all blubbing so much they didn't understand what he was talking about, but the Boss got the message and quickly crossed his name off the Christmas Card List.

Talking of Christmas Cards, did you see Margaret's favourite poem she quoted in Women's Realm? You might like to know that it came off a card she got last year from Maurice's Antique Hypermarket lady:

> When skies above are dark and grey
> And troubles get you down
> A smile will chase your cares away
> And soon replace your frown.

Try saying it when you've had a few. I find it jolly moving.
Yours in tears,

DENIS

10 Downing Street
Whitehall

14 December 1984

Dear Bill,

I was sorry to hear that Maurice came a cropper over the Telecom issue and had his application sent back. But I do wish he would refrain from ringing me up on these occasions in such a highly emotional condition, especially as he knows full well that relations between Number Ten and Number Eleven, at least between the menfolk, are decidedly frosty. Even so, with the Yuletide nearly on us, I did poke my nose around the door in a charitable manner and ask what was up. Old friend, good war record, scraped together his savings to have a flutter, usher in the new age of shareholder democracy, only to receive bum's rush. Lawson, who obviously thought it was me and not my friend at all, turned up his enormous hooter in the usual snooty fashion and said that thousands of other entries had been disqualified on technical points to do with the application form. 'And if you will insist on doing your paper work after lunch, Denis' – this with a great smirk and his waistcoat going up and down as he chuckled – 'you have no one to blame but yourself.'

As you may have seen, the Mad Monk is under sedation after being duffed over by Margaret's Bovver Boot Boys. It's often baffled me why the crinkly-haired old loon soldiers on, especially when every time he sticks his head out of the door he gets pelted with a couple of dozen standard, medium or large. However there has always been a strange rapport between him and my better half, going back to the time when she entered the ring against Sailor Ted with the Monk in her corner flapping the wet towel. His latest wheeze for once seemed reasonably sound. You know my view about students: layabouts, troublemakers, unwashed fornicators and dope-fiends living it up at my expense and yours in agreeable listed buildings. Why not, the Monk reasoned in a rare moment of lucidity, make the parents of these long-haired slugs cough up a goodly whack towards their breakages, magistrates' fines etc?

Shrill squeals might have been expected at this from the Moscow-funded Smellysocks, but no one had anticipated any trouble from our own side. What they don't realise of course is that with a swing like they had last time, the place has filled up with some of the most grisly detritus of common little yoiks ever seen on the Tory back benches, all of them keen to cash in on anything that's going, all wanting their spotty offspring turned into gentlemen scientists and upwardly mobile computer programmers. Not surprisingly, the prospect of having to put their hands in their own pockets to this end soon had them up on their hind legs, baying for the blood of the Monk.

Meanwhile Herself was being implanted by helicopter into Dublin Castle for yet another Euro Pissup, suitably hosted by my cork-sniffing friend Dr FitzG. After announcing that she couldn't understand why there had been all this talk of her being inflexible with the Teasock she hurried off for various intimate tete-a-tetes with her new boyfriend Monsieur Maurice Garlic-Breath Chevalier, the President of the French Republic. Their little tiff about contributions is now forgotten and it's all kissy kissy to a fairly nauseating degree. They're even talking about building the Channel Tunnel a.s.a.p. so they can see even more of each other, Old MacGregor to be redeployed in charge of the excavations. Imagine her shock then, as they sat toasting one another in Spanish Burgundy, to receive news of the Monk being stuck in a corner at Halitosis Hall with the Skinheads sinking

'. . . *fumbling with a big bottle of green pills* . . .'

their teeth in his legs. Not only that but Sailorboy Ted had once again taken advantage of her absence to heave himself out of his hammock and perform a pretty terrible pantomime routine with himself as Mother Goose poking fun at her scheme to abolish the Red Brigade at County Hall.

I don't know which was worse for the poor old Monk; being debagged by the yoiks or getting the laser beam treatment from Queen Boadicea in one of her chillier moods. I met him in the corridor coming out of the study, fumbling with a big bottle of green pills and muttering to himself about making a terrible mistake and having to atone for it. He clearly had no idea who I was. It crossed my mind to propose a stiffener but remembering what happened to Maurice when he washed his Uppers down with a tumblerful of neat Pernod I let him pass. All to no avail as he proceeded to slosh the contents of the pill-bottle back with a large G and T and stumbled out through the front door, where needless to say a quorum of egg-chuckers was waiting for a spot of target practice.

Christmas comes on apace. I did ask little Brittan off the record if he could get the boy Mark's re-entry permit chewed up in the computer, but I fear we may have to grin and bear it.

Stay low (some chance!),

DENIS

10 Downing Street
Whitehall

28 DECEMBER 1984

Dear Bill,

I'm sorry you couldn't join Maurice, myself and his Antique Lady when they came up for their last-minute Christmas Shopping spree. Probably just as well under the circs. The idea was to R.V. at the R.A.C. mid-morning and then sally forth to Regent Street to find a few stocking-fillers for the nearest and dearest, take in a light lunch at Selfridges, load up a taxi with our purchases and then back to Number Ten for fortified tea before popping the happy couple on the Flying Wino back to Dover Priory.

Alas, events fell out otherwise. Our first mistake in my view was to accept a seasonal snort in the Ladies Annexe from that awful buffoon Frank Longford, who has taken to coming into the Club to use the swimming pool. Maurice's Antique Lady took a tremendous shine to Old Baldy, sat on his lap and told him he was a bit of all right. Maurice naturally got very shirty about this and asked Longford to step outside. I said why didn't we all step outside and get on with the shopping but then suddenly they became very friendly and decided on one for the road, followed by a splash in the pool to cool off. By the time they got back to the Bar they seemed to have lost Longford but claimed their teeth

49

were chattering and ordered trebles. Next thing I remember the Club Secretary was having a word in my ear to say that there had been complaints from Members about our lady guest standing on the table in the library to sing carols. By this time the restaurant was closed, the usual mob in the bar were in jocular mood, and the prospect of getting our heads down in the scrum at Lilly-white's began to seem less and less attractive. Maurice became very matey with a pretty shifty looking old cove under the impression that they'd been in the R.A.S.C. together, his lady disappeared to powder her nose and that was the last we saw of her. I myself struck lucky, as I thought at the time, in that I ran into a bloke who'd just taken delivery of a consignment of cut-price hampers from Fortnum's: no questions asked, cash in hand, drop them off by plain van later that night. As I recall I handed over a monkey in readies, only to discover next morning that the damn fool had tried to deliver at Number Eleven and got a flea in his ear from Mother Lawson. Like Maurice's lady he has not been seen since.

As you may gather from the foregoing mousey adventures the cat has been away, whistle-stopping round the globe a la Super-woman, girdling the planet in a matter of moments. I couldn't see the point of it quite frankly, as she could have easily signed away Hong Kong to Mr Dung by Telex and bending Hopalong's ear might have been done a great deal more effectively over the blower, deaf though he be. Shouting would have been consider-ably simpler than all that air-travel. Originally it was ordained that I too was to tag along. However you may have seen that we played host to Mr Gorblimov and his very presentable Missus. (Don't ask me why. Six months ago it was a non-speaks situation with the Bear, source of all evil in the universe etc., suddenly it's all hunky-dory, lunch out at some derelict pile beyond Wimbledon, Howe slobbering over the snow-covered boots of Yesterday's Enemy as if he was a human being.) Anyway, when I was introduced I naturally asked the interpreter why Comrade G. was wasting his time with our lot, when his friend Arthur Scargill was no doubt keeping a fish and chip lunch hot for him on the picket lines and expecting his usual cheque from Moscow Narodny Bank. I could see the interpreter blanch a bit at this, and Margaret immediately jumped in to divert the conversation onto heavy engineering. Later I was told brusquely by an aide that my presence would not after all be required on the jaunt to Honkers. I did my best to look upset.

'. . . followed by a splash in the pool to cool off . . .'

Before leaving, the Boss went on the TV to blast the Wets, doing her Mrs Scrooge act and saying that in future there would be no more free handouts to school-leavers, no going back, blood, sweat, toil, tears and champagne corks cracking in the boardroom. But if you ask me the yoiks on the back benches have tasted blood. No sooner was her back turned than Jenkin was being debagged to universal cheering.

You are very wise to spend Christmas in Lanzarote, even if, as you say, you don't intend to put a foot outside the door. Remember me as you knock back the Pina Coladas, enduring the pains of Purgatory in the bosom of the family round the tree at Chequers. We are once again threatened with the Howes on Boxing Day. And Mr Munster is coming to stay for an open-ended convalescence. I suppose that's something to look forward to.

Yours while life lingers,

DENIS

10 Downing Street
Whitehall

8 FEBRUARY 1985

Dear Bill,

I am amazed by what you tell me about the Major putting it round the Club that the lapse in our correspondence was due to my having been 'dispatched to dry out at Broadlands'. The fact is that following this Ponting business, the Boss has instituted a major security blackout, with the result that even my private correspondence has been gone through by two buggers in trench coats who have obviously fed my last two screeds into the shredder. Not that there was anything remotely sensitive in them, other than a few offensive remarks about Lawson. Talking of whom, I couldn't resist rubbing his nose in it a bit when the solids hit the airconditioning last week over the OPEC circus. Fatty had been trotting round saying the pound would find its own level, everything tickety-boo, never fear, Skipper Nigel at the helm etc, when Wham, slap into the iceberg, lifeboat stations and arse-end out of the water. I was fortunate enough to collide with him as he sidled into Number Ten for Correction with Madame T. and made some jocular reference to his navigational skills. 'What of your famous Tax Cuts the noo?' At this he purpled up no end, stuck his nose in the air, made an odd snorting noise, and ponced off to take his medicine.

If truth be told, 14% is pretty good news to those of us who've got a bit under the bed for a rainy day, but I obviously couldn't tell him that.

You would have thought, at this stage, with our lot hacking about in the rough, that little Kinnock would have seized his chance to sink a putt or twain. Not a bit of it. Smellysocks put down some frightful-sounding censure motion, all channels of communication booked for a full-scale coverage, but as usual little Ginger Pillock having danced into the ring and sparred about for a few seconds was stopped in his tracks by the Grantham Gouger and left looking like a piece of knotted string. As I said to Maurice in the House of Lords Snug afterwards, they should all take a leaf out of old Snaggleteeth Stockton's book. He may be a hundred and six, but he certainly knows how to put the boot in. I don't know whether you saw his performance on Geriatrics' Half Hour. Personally I thought it was a lot of piss and wind, but he had Boris sobbing into his vodka like a child.

A propos the Senior Citizens, Boris tells me that poor old MacGregor is now kept in padded accommodation somewhere near Clacton to stop him shooting his mouth off. Like Maurice's friend from Broadstairs Hazel Pinder-White, who as you may have seen has been making a bit of an ass of herself suing young Aitken in the High Court, the Boss is determined come what may to have Friend Scargill on his knees on the beach begging for mercy, and will brook no interference from MacGregor or anyone else that might prevent her enjoying that moment of triumph.

You ask if the Boss was miffed when the Oxford egg-heads black-balled her from their Funny Hats and Gowns Club. I happen to know that when the idea was first mooted by some young brown-tonguer from the dreaming spires, the Boss became quite misty-eyed; in fact I distinctly remember the scene at the breakfast table when she dropped the EPNS with a clatter in mid-egg. 'I little thought, Denis, as I biked out to the Labs all those years ago as plain Margaret Roberts that I should one day return to Oxford to receive the highest honour that our greatest university can bestow. An Honorary Degree in the Sheldonian Theatre.' At the time I refrained from pointing out that these old codgers distribute honours of this nature with a packet of corn-flakes to every tin-pot coon and mafioso who takes the trouble to check in at the Randolph. Even I myself, if you remember, had to go and dress up in some damnfool dressing-gown and cowpat hat at Peebles when I was on the board at Burmah to be made an honorary Doctor of Applied Lubricants. However the Boss had obviously set her heart on the Oxford Accolade and had even got the little woman round the corner to run up a frock to go with the outfit. If you ask me she also had half an eye on the prospect of getting her own back on old Stockton who in his role as Chancellor would have had to parade through the streets at her side trying to look as though he was enjoying it. Instead of which some band of barmy Lefties and long-haired Trots got up a protest motion at the last minute and scuppered it.

I was all for pulling the rug from under those fat cats with their sherry parties and eight-course dinners pretty sharpish and letting the Monk loose to make a few judicious cuts. I ventured to suggest as much to the Boss but she claimed to have forgotten all

'. . . an honorary Doctor of Applied Lubricants . . .'

about it and said that Oxford had always been a hotbed of Communism even in her day; it was of no concern whatever to her, these tinsel honours were meaningless, she was too busy running the country etc. All very well, but if you ask me it was not a coincidence when that same evening the wild-eyed Rasputin de nos jours was summoned round to discuss annual MOTs for all university lecturers, with special reference to those working in large car-manufacturing towns within a sixty mile radius of London.

Are your Americans still coming over on Thursdays to do their marketing? If so I could warn Lillywhite's to lay in some of their electric buggies with the cocktail cabinet attachment. If they felt like taking half a dozen we might even get a commission on it.

Yours in the spirit of enterprise,

DENIS

10 Downing Street
Whitehall

Dear Bill,

Very glad to hear you missed my brief moment of TV glory during the Ten Years as Tory Leader anniversary photo-call at Number Ten. The whole shooting match was got up as a multi-media advertising presentation by the Corsican Twins, the brothers Saatchi, and as per usual the reptiles were up to their monkey tricks. When the Boss had done her bit about how much she loved it and how keenly she was looking forward to another ten years, one of the little vermin called out 'What about you then, Den? Will you be cracking open the bubbly ten years from now?' I said not if I could bloody well help it, at which M. got very shirty and giving me a blast of the gamma rays said 'Of course he will. Just his little joke.' Public humiliation of poor old D.T. enjoyed by millions, cold tongue pie for lunch, forty-eight hours confined to barracks, on parade every 10 minutes in full battle order, cookhouse fatigues and nil by mouth for the duration.

As it transpired the celebration was an utter washout thanks to the Communist infiltrator Mr Priggy Ponting, a little Trot from the Min. of Def., presumably on the official payroll of the Kremlin like Scargill. Havers, the fun-loving Attorney General, who you may remember we bumped into once in the Purple Pussy Club in Old Compton Street on one of our nights of mischief when the Boss was away, had assured Margaret that Ponting's goose was well and truly cooked – judge briefed, jury one hundred per cent Tory voters, all the trimmings. But as usual where the gentlemen of the law are concerned, old Grogblossom had ballsed it up and some rabid revolutionary hag from County Hall slipped through the net and swung the wrong verdict, much to the delight of the Smellysocks, the reptiles and all the forces of darkness, thus allowing the little bugger to escape his just desserts, i.e. a good long spell breaking rocks at Her Majesty's pleasure.

The Boss, needless to say, was apoplectic with rage and settled down to a spell of carpet chewing before summoning Heseltine and Havers for the piano wire treatment. What really riled her

'. . . *we bumped into at the Purple Pussy Club . . .*'

was not being able to sound off in public against the twelve good men and true, it being the accepted wisdom that such a quorum represents the last bastion of democracy and freedom. Whereas you and I know from respective spells of duty in Tunbridge Wells and Tenterden, that they are an ignorant rabble of pressed morons whose only interest is in telling each other dirty stories and ensuring that the whole thing's sewn up by opening time at the Frog and Loincloth.

Just when things were looking really ugly little Pillock came to the rescue yet again by accusing the Boss of masterminding the prosecution of Master Priggy. This was all the old girl needed for a really good scrap, Sylvester v. Tweetie-Pie Kinnock, the latter handicapped yet again by the loss of his voice and the need to be swallowing Fisherman's Friends every ten seconds to make himself heard above the roar of the brawling winos on the back benches. Following the predictable flutter of yellow feathers, M. as Pussycat Sylvester then insisted that the freckled Tweetie-Pie must say sorry before she would allow him back on his perch.

Having lost his voice, Pillock was reduced to putting his thoughts on paper, in my experience with the Boss an ill-advised move, as however strong one's case she somehow manages to twist the sense to her advantage. He bombarded the Boss with poison pen letters, saying she had lied in her teeth, no apology from him, yah boo sucks etc., all of which was given prominence on the front pages of the various gutter sheets. Eventually the Red Canary had to concede that he had got it wrong, but he was damned if he was going to say sorry. The Proprietor was still very miffed and his name has been duly entered in the hate book alongside Brother Scargill.

Entre nous, though I haven't given voice to this opinion in the matrimonial home, I think Margaret's story about having been on holiday with the Widow Glover when the whole thing blew up is pretty good eyewash. Of course she may not have signed the actual charge sheet, but don't tell me that Havers and Co. didn't twig that nothing would delight the old girl more than Ponting's head on a charger delivered personally to Number Ten by Inter-Bonce.

A propos, I saw your friend and neighbour Alan Clark put his foot in it with the Pinkos by suggesting that certain ethnic minorities were worried about being shipped back 'to Bongo Bongo Land'. It seems to me that things have come to a pretty pass if a chap can't make a perfectly sensible observation of that nature without being called upon to withdraw by prats like Runcie and the Guardian. Talking of Runcie, if you were watching the Synod on TV as I was, you will have seen that he totally failed to administer a wigging to the Durham Godbotherer. Instead of speaking out as Archie Wellbeloved would have done and ordering him to be burned at the stake, Runcie made his usual bleat about there being good points on both sides and just because you burn down the goal posts it doesn't mean you're not a loyal member of the Fifteen. Give me Crufts any day.

I remain,
'Her Greatest Fan',
(as seen on TV),

DENIS

P.S. Hats off to Tarzan for his Arnhem-style midnight drop at Molesworth to shift the long-haired conchies, what?

10 Downing Street
Whitehall

8 MARCH 1985

Dear Bill,

I'm sorry to hear that Daphne wasn't amused by my prezzo from the US of A. I wasn't suggesting for a moment that either of you had AIDS, but these do-it-yourself detector kits are selling like hot cakes in the Big Apple, and I thought you'd be amused by the little rubber gloves. Why don't you forward it anonymously to that curate you were telling me about who made a pass at Maurice in the Long Room?

I'm afraid the Special Relationship beano was a bit of a dead duck. The old girl was absolutely over the moon, bless her heart, when they invited her to be the first British P.M. since Winston to talk in their equivalent of Halitosis Hall. (I can never remember which is the Senate and which is the Congress, I don't suppose it matters very much.) Anyway, the Corsican Brothers laid on a team of copy-writers including Sir Custardface, armed with the Reader's Digest Golden Treasurehouse of Wit and Wisdom, little Gordon Grease was choppered in to add herbs and spices to the brew, I was driven round to Harley Street for a tough talking to from Bosendorfer's friend Dr Gropius about loss of self- esteem and mixing with social inferiors and handed a milk-bottle full of the Antibooze pills Maurice used to take, which I of course flushed down the loo the moment I got back to H.Q.

'. . . a tough talking to from Doctor Gropius . . .'

I had hoped the flight to Washington would include a Western with suitable Ambassador Class refreshments, but the Captain told me the Boss had ordered all the seats and the bar unit to be taken out so that she could rehearse her speech without the distraction of revelling winos from the Cabinet Office.

Hopalong was waiting on the tarmac with the red carpet and the customary damnfool drum majorettes prancing up and down: the anorexic spouse was clutching his paw as usual, and dropped a curtsey to the Boss obviously thinking she was someone else. The old boy himself seemed to have had another couple of tucks taken out of his face since we last met, and his hair is now ox-blood. The next day we all filed in to the Washington H.H., and I must say the Boss got a very nice round of applause from the white-haired cowpunchers and Colonel Sanders lookalikes there assembled. She then stepped onto the rostrum and gave them forty minutes' worth of what they fancied, references to Sir Winston, Dark Days of the War, Yellow Peril, Red Menace, Hands across the Sea, bung everything into space including the kitchen sink, U.S. know-how an inspiration to the entire world etc.

I could see some of the old grandpappies sobbing into their bandanas, and everything seemed to be entirely tickety-boo. The whole point of all this, as you will have realised, was to butter up Hopalong to such an extent that she could then twist his arm on letting some steam out of the dollar, at present putting the kibosh on all Mr Nicely Nicely Lawson's Springtime Tax Cuts. At a suitable moment therefore as she was receiving congratulations in her dressing room afterwards, M. took him aside and explained her dilemma, how the high price of the dollar was threatening her stability and could lead to a Communist Government in Britain, headed by Kinnock. The old ham seemed to be drinking it all in, his face registering grandfatherly concern, compassionate twitch of an eyebrow, arm round the shoulders and so on. However, no sooner were our backs turned than he went on Coast to Coast television to say they hadn't seen nothing yet, the dollar was going to ride even higher and those who were squealing had nobody but themselves to blame. As you can imagine, the Boss, who had been expecting a rapturous welcome home from her historic mission with the dollar obediently tumbling on arrival, was pretty sore at having browned her tongue in vain. The Smellysocks were quick to rub her face in it, and the old girl took it all very badly, saying she had been cruelly let down and that it was distressing to find one's hero not only had feet of clay but also played a pretty dirty game of poker. Personally I put it down to general deterioration of the grey cells. The old boy I'm sure had meant to do his bit, but he clearly can't retain anything for more than a few moments, and as their conversation wasn't in the minutes it probably went clean out of his mind on the way to the TV studio. We had the same trouble with that Chairman at Burmah who used to blow bubbles at Board Meetings and always had odd socks on.

The Boss's revenge is to be taken on the Barnsley Lenin, King Arthur. For the first time in years the tramp of hob-nailed boots was heard in the hall, and the new leader of the horny-handed sons of toil Mr Willis and his cohorts came round for the old traditional beer and smoked salmon sandwiches. The Boss was surprisingly polite, and told them that she greatly valued their views on any topic. Willis and his chums were obviously a bit bewildered by this, having expected the usual fire-breathing dragon act and a lecture about the need for hard work. While they were still groggy from the shock Walker produced a form of words to settle the strike and said he was grateful to them for having drawn it up and that he was sure he himself could agree to a good deal of it. Still stunned they were then shunted out the front door and exposed to the reptiles for a group photo. This in turn made Arthur livid at being left out, and he retreated to his bunker. However finally on Sunday even he had to admit defeat and come out with the white flag flying. The Boss decreed that there was to be no talk of any victory but since then the champagne corks have been popping non-stop.

Boris was very upset about this phone-tapping business. He says it's not only the CND and the Lefties who are under surveillance: according to a conversation with little Brittan he monitored only the other day, you and I are being bugged all round the clock and the transcripts are passed round MI5 to much sniggering from the Ponting Brigade. Could this explain why Daphne came home unexpectedly last Friday?

Yours sub rosa,

DENIS

10 Downing Street
Whitehall
22 MARCH 1985

Dear Bill,
You enquire why no national junketings following Comrade Scargill's fifty-nil defeat at the hands of my good lady the Grantham Mauler. That was precisely my reaction. You'd think that after a year spending millions on well and truly humiliating the wretched little Bolshie, the least they could do would be to blow a couple of thou on a really good celebration, be it in the form of a whole holiday for schools, a Thanksgiving Service at St Paul's with Runcie under lock and key, or possibly a firework display with Arthur burned in effigy.

To be fair to the Boss, she agreed with me that such a scenario was in order. Enter then however the Corsican Twins, Alberto y Luigi, flourishing the results of their overnight market research, which purported to show that the Boss's shelf-life would be drastically reduced were she to indulge in any such exercise. Selected housewives had been asked for their opinion, and they all plumped for a kiss and make-up reconciliation between the warring factions, and a low-key business-as-usual pay-off. In view of the shrivelling pound and Kinnock's ten-point lead in the polls this eventually won approval.

It didn't stop me, I may say, from funding my own private beano down at the Club, where a lot of the boys got pretty tight and set fire to some of the soft furnishings.

I imagine poor old Hopalong must be rather feeling the draught now that Chernenko has turned his toes up. The one thing that kept him going all these years was the thought that however senile he may be, his opposite number at the Kremlin has always hitherto been allotted the bed nearest the door. Now the Russkies, pretty sozzled and never very quick off the mark, have finally hauled in the fact that things proceed rather more smoothly if the Chairman of the Board can at least find his way to the Gents without assistance. The upshot is that instead of another incontinent OAP they have handed the baton to a younger bugger, one Comrade Gorblimoff, who you remember toddling over here recently to see the sights, bringing with him a very nifty little wife and making a great impression on the Boss, who can spot a fellow bone-crusher miles off.

Naturally she leapt at the idea of climbing once again into her Moscow Funeral Outfit, which is beginning to look a bit shiny at the elbows, to be there as Most Favoured Foreign Dignitary while they were wheeling the stiff round Red Square to the strains of solemn music. A further inducement for M. to shine as the funeral baked meats were being snapped up in the Hall of Mirrors was that poor old Hoppo failed to show, the official word being unavoidable business engagements – the truth, if you ask me, was that the medicos rightly advised that three hours standing to attention in minus thirty degrees while they rolled past every available jalopyful of rockets in their arsenal could well sound the old fellow's death knell.

Frankly, after the fiasco of Mother Gandhi's send-off I didn't fancy sharing a mini-bus with Kinnock and Steel, so I usefully filled in the time by tooling down to the Major's Bring and Buy in

'. . . *funding my own private beano down at the club* . . .'

aid of Police Horse Trainers, and got in a few rounds at Rye with Archie Wellbeloved's brother, the one who was drummed out of that Prep School at Broadstairs for allegedly jumping too low in the leapfrog. Don't say I'm not a tolerant man – though personally I never believed the story and have always found him a very sociable bloke when it comes to knocking back the doubles until four-thirty a.m. in the Residents' Lounge.

As you probably saw, Sailor Ted has been let out of his basket again, making his customary snide observations, this time on the TV. If you ask me, our chubby friend was extremely miffed about the Boss's victory over the Miners, particularly in view of the fact that that was where he came unstuck himself. I suppose the thought has also crossed his mind that he's not getting any younger and that he'd better put his best foot forward, ideally up the arse of the leadership, if any hope of a comeback is to be entertained before the Chernenko phase sets in. I know what he feels like.

Hope you managed to get the consignment below decks before Mr Nicely Nicely slapped his new price labels on.

Yours to the bitter end,

DENIS

10 Downing Street
Whitehall

5 APRIL 1985

Dear Bill,

A propos the Budget, I am as delighted as you are to see the smile wiped off the face of our fat friend from Number 11. A year ago, you may recall, the sun shone from out of his fundament, causing Margaret to don her dark glasses whenever he held forth and mark him down as a dangerous rival on a par with Tarzan and Mr Munster for the take-over stakes. Now, at a stroke, as our seafaring friend E. Heath used to say, the Golden Boy has become the dunce in the corner, and Ladbroke's won't give you much more than 100 to 1 on his finishing in the first four.

I couldn't resist rubbing his nose in it a bit when I espied him over the garden wall taking one of his sprogs to task for insubordination. 'Sorry about your getting boxed in,' I called, 'no doubt we shall have to wait till next year for the tax cuts you were telling us about.' This provoked one of his predictable jibes about me having to go and drown my sorrows at the R.A.C., but I thought it was Advantage D.T., especially as his sprog kicked him in the shin just as I toddled off to follow his advice.

Talking of Mr Munster, word round the Power House is that the wretched little creeping Jesus of the Lower Fourth, Gummer, is about to get the boot with ten minutes' notice to clear his desk. I never liked him since he handed me a tract at Blackpool with a disgusting caricature of a decrepit wino staggering down the Primrose Path and a spruce teetotaller in a bowler hat and pin-stripe smugly ascending the Hill Difficult to the Heavenly City. Sod him. His place is to be taken by Mr Munster, who is trying to mellow from punk bother boy into kindly avuncular patriarch, cracking jokes and handing out fivers to the children of party workers. Not a role, I may say, that comes naturally to our Norman, but he toddled in for a screw-driver or twain the other night when Margaret was slumming it out in the sticks and told me, when Boris went out of the room for a moment, that he was very impressed by my own personal image and asked whether I had any tips on how to win a reputation for bonhomie. I said the secret, like the Genie, was to be found in the bottle.

You'll be pleased to hear, a propos Margaret's intended reshuffle, that she has finally seen the light about her dancing partner from the Bromley Charm School, friend Cecil, who will not after all be asked back on the bus, where he once gave her the benefit of his aftershave and obsequious smiles. The powers that be have decided that despite his gifts as a TV salesperson, he is a bit too rich for the pudding. No great loss in my view, but the Boss shed a few quiet tears into her hankie after she crossed his name off the list, and said it was a tragic case of a man brought down by a fatal weakness – glancing sternly at myself as she spoke.

As you can see from the foregoing, some of our chaps here have got the wind up, following Mr Nicely's lamentable performance with the battered leather case. Kinnock's personal rating has leaped ahead, which says something for the state we're in. The Corsican Brothers, having completely buggered up the Victory Celebrations after the Miners' Strike by advocating a low-key

'. . . who ladled out a plateful of fancies . . .'

softly-softly scenario, proceeded to recommend to Margaret that she should demonstrate her great concern for the plight of the unwaged by entertaining a charabanc full of pimply Scouse layabouts to tea and cucumber sandwiches at Downing Street. I myself was told to be on hand to provide light relief and keep an eye on the silver. At the outset, all seemed pretty much under control. The yobbos filed in, rubber-necking round at the fixtures and fittings, and were ushered upstairs to the drawing room, where Boris was standing by the tea-urn, assisted by a couple of old bags from Charlie Forte's outfit, who ladled out a plateful of fancies and they all went off, sat on the edge of their chairs and munched away. The Boss then blew it. Never keen on anyone getting something for nothing, she delivered a stern lecture on the need for them all to get off their fat arses and start window-cleaning or set up multi-million pound computer businesses. Whereupon they all fell out of the front door snarling and growling, much to the delight of the reptiles who were waiting with microphones at the ready to record their thoughts.

I couldn't agree more about Brer Leon copping out completely on the TV Licence Fee. You'd think the least thing this lot could do would be to crack down once and for all on that nest of raving Bolshies and free-loading pansies at the BBC, instead of which Joe Soap has to stump up another twelve quid a year for the privilege of being lectured by a lot of queasy-looking red stooges on the joys of life behind the Iron Curtain. I'd be perfectly happy to settle for the old black and white but you can't see the ball very well when they drive off, particularly if it's after lunch. And the snooker makes no sense whatsoever.

Did the Major or Maurice get on to you about our proposed weekend of thwacking the pill in Rye? I'm told the Mermaid is full of Americans, but there's a very jolly little woman called Polly Carter-Ruck who does B&B at Appledore. Own front door key, no questions asked. Does this appeal?

DENIS

10 Downing Street
Whitehall
19 APRIL 1985

Dear Bill,
Wasn't there some story or other about a chap in the olden days who went whizzing round the world in a balloon for a bet and was so dazed when he got back that he didn't realise what day it was, let alone that the Club Bar was still open? I can't remember how it turned out, but I can quite understand how the poor old cove felt. I woke up at three o'clock this morning, got dressed and bowled down to the R.A.C. for lunch. I thought first of all it was a rather murky sort of day, not many people about, but when I got there

the Night Porter very decently took me into his box and administered a tranquillising draught of Jap whisky from the jerry-can under his chair. It was then I realised that my body-clock, as the medics call it, had gone on the blink.

Not that one can blame it in the circs. You ask what was achieved apart from knocking a good five years off one's natural span? The answer, as far as I'm concerned, is sweet F.A., or sweet F.O. might be nearer the mark. As you know, these trips are all hatched over the duty-free vodka by the reds and weirdos at the Foreign Office on a Saturday morning when they haven't got much to do. No earthly purpose is served, but the Boss can't resist a chance to rip off her tweeds and twinset, revealing the Wonderwoman leotard and cloak, and circle the globe in a shower of sparks.

As you can well imagine, I did my best to be excused the exercise, pleading an important business lunch at the Savoy with Maurice P. and his boy Kevin who is setting up some kind of dental equipment emporium in the Mile End Road. However the powers that be dictated otherwise, and in the end I think this was probably a good thing. It's usually me who doesn't know which day of the week it is, but on this occasion the old girl dropped a trail of clangers rather in the style of old Prosser-Cluff in his butter-flicking period. At one point when she began to hail the achievements of the brave Indonesian people while addressing the Singapore Businesswomen's Anti-Communist League, or it may have been the other way round, I felt obliged to lean forward and put her right on her geography. Not that I got a word of thanks, and indeed took a full dose of gamma rays while the oriental ladies tittered nervously into their hankies.

Talking of Prosser-Cluff, I mentioned his name to Mr Lee, the very sensible little man who runs Singapore, knowing that he shared with P-C a liking for a round of golf and a toughish line with the Unions. Lee's face immediately lit up and he paid a glowing tribute to the man who had brought the workers to heel by setting fire to their living quarters, and repeated what I had heard before, i.e. that they all adored him for it. It was at this stage, I think, that the Boss got rather carried away and made a fiery speech extolling Mr Lee as the hammer of the Trots, venturing to boast of her own achievements in settling the hash of Friend Scargill. Naturally the reptiles picked it up, and the Smellysocks, desperate for anything to throw into the stew, immediately made the most of it. (On that topic, I'd like to see

'. . . obliged to feed the sacred elephants . . .'

Brother Kaufmann attempt the Nineteen Cities of the Orient in Four Days Dash. One blast of hot air off the tarmac and Baldie would melt into his terylene tropical suiting.) Not but what the travelling media circus, ever on the look-out for a bone to chew, immediately started bombarding the Boss with namby-pamby comments from him and the other whining pinkos at home, accusing her of selling the British worker down the river and crying stinking fish in someone else's back yard. Margaret's answer, which these morons didn't seem to grasp, was that your wily oriental businessman has been under the impression for years that this country is inhabited by a rabble of work-shy Trots living off the state, with barely sufficient energy to heave back the blanket and toddle down to the corner to pick up the dole. You and I know that nothing has changed, but the Boss is trying to push the line that the old firm is now under New Management, and Scargill's bleeding head is held up as an example of what happens to those who don't like it. A point well worth making, in my view, considering the hopeless balls-up that the Corsican Twins made of our Victory in the Pits.

This unseemly controversy apart, I came back with my respect for the good old D of E very much enhanced. Having watched twenty-six displays of Native Dancing, shaken hands with four hundred and fifty-three diplomats and their wives and even been obliged to feed a suitably engraved coconut to the sacred elephants, I now realise there is more to being a Royal than meets the inexperienced eye. By the way, did you see that barmy Scotsman in the Sunday Express suggested I should be given a peerage for my pains? I was rather touched by that, quite frankly. But if you'd spent any time in the Bar at the House of Lords, you'd share my reluctance to don the ermine. You may think the R.A.C. has some pretty hard cases, but that gaggle of geriatric winos at half-past ten in the morning trying to pick up their tonic bottles make you, me and Maurice look like outpatients.

I brought you back one or two exotic curiosities which came by Diplomatic Bag. I don't want Daphne to see them particularly, so I'll wait until our lunch at the Praying Dog in Tonbridge on the 20th.

Yours garlanded with flowers,
DENIS

10 Downing Street
Whitehall

3 MAY 1985

Dear Bill,
I'm glad we see eye to eye about the Princess Michael business. As you rightly surmised, it was all got up by a grubby little nest of Trots round at the Daily Mirror. And I also happen to know that Robert Maxwell is very thick with the Kremlin and has already

signed up Gorblimov to write his memoirs. So it doesn't require much second sight to see what's going on, i.e. the discrediting of the Royal Family as a last desperate bid, after the failure of Scargill, to bring about violent revolution.

I felt I had to write to poor old Reibnitz's girl, spelling it out for her, because sometimes these people are a bit out of touch with the political realities and take it personally. As it happens I had a bit of an 'in' with the distaff side of the Kent set-up, having bumped into the Baron a couple of times on business in South Africa. He always seemed to me to be a perfectly decent old cove, very sound on the Red Menace, labour relations, the welfare state, etc. He was very pally with old Mrs Keffirbesher Senior, as he was with many of the good ladies on the Joburg circuit, where he was known as the Baron von Randypants. Of course the word was that he'd been mixed up with the Ribbentrop lot, but as I understand it his main interest was bagging the local wild life, plus any Russky trouble-makers who happened to cross his sights, and what better recommendation could one have than that? I remember one particular evening at Mrs K's under the stars when the Baron had had a few and got rather weepy about the old days, saying that if only Winnie and Adolf hadn't been so touchy we could all have joined forces in '45 and flattened the Reds once and for all.

Of course no one's seriously suggesting that the Palace didn't know about this all along. For a start most of the D of E's relatives were on the other side, mixing cocktails for the German High Command. No reason at all therefore for them to blackball Prince Michael for going through with it. All the same I didn't think he made a frightfully good showing on this occasion. After all, if in a purely hypothetical case, the Boss were to be ostracised as the daughter of a raving Grantham Mosleyite, I think the least I could have done would be to toddle along to TV-AM and sit beside her on the sofa, nodding supportively while she made her tearful appeal to the nation for sympathy.

By the way, what price poor old Devonshire being caught with his trousers down? Now we know why he had to sell off the family portraits, with all these floozies expecting to be showered with flowers and chocolates every hour of the day. Personally, I've always got on very well with him. We both share an interest in liquid refreshment, and in my experience he never allowed women to get in the way of it. But there we are, still waters run deep.

Enough of this social chit-chat. M's been up to her arse in

'. . . the Baron got rather weepy about the old days . . .'

crocodiles thanks to our fat friend next door at Number Eleven.
His latest plan is to crack down on the layabouts and pensioners
in the terminal wards in order to raise money for his tax bonanza
for the likes of us. A perfectly sound scheme on paper, but
brother Nigel has about as much finesse as the Major on a bad
night, with the result that little Fowler has gone whimpering to
M, and at the last minute, with local elections looming and Taffy

Kinnock rising in the charts, the whole thing's had to be momentarily shelved with red faces all round.

Hopalong, as you may have observed, is no longer Flavour of the Month. No doubt moved by the plight of Princess Michael, the old movie star took it into his head to celebrate VE Day being filmed laying a wreath on the Tomb of the Unknown SS Man during his forthcoming trip to Krautland. Needless to say this went down like a lead balloon with the New York fraternity, and the Boss, who in view of her setbacks was feeling like putting the high heel in somewhere along the line decided that Hoppo had had it coming to him for a long time, and blasted his so-called reconciliation bid from the Front Bench at Question Time.

Talking of that sort of thing, we were hoping to have a reunion of the Veterans' Lodge at the Savoy on VE Day itself. The plan was to get Bomber Harris to say grace, but now he's turned his toes up we're a bit stuck. Whiffy Heatherington suggested Runcie, but I trod on that p.d.q. despite the fact that Rev. Snaggleteeth in his day was no mean slayer of the Boche. What about that old Chindit you ran into in Folkestone who had spent time inside for pyromania? I'm sure if we had a word with Wontner and told the waiters to keep him out of reach of the matches he'd do the job as well as anybody.

Give us a bell to let me know your thinking on this.

Sieg Heil from all of us here in the Bunker,

DENIS

 10 Downing Street
Whitehall

17 MAY 1985

Dear Bill,

What a wonderful celebration of my 70th! I may say that when I received Maurice's invitation to address the East Sussex Small Businessmen's Association on 'Some Experiences on and off the Rugby Football Field', I never twigged for an instant what lay behind it. Right up to the moment when I took my place on the platform next to the Padre and the curtains were drawn aside to raucous cheering from the DT Fan Club and the Bells' Yew

Green Footwarmers struck up 'Where Shall We Be A Hundred Years From Now?' I seriously believed a bona fide evening of decorous boredom lay ahead with little more in prospect than half a bottle of Cyprus Sherry.

Of course you were perfectly right in thinking that I'd never have been let off the leash, had the Boss herself known the true nature of the beano. I fear that even so she may suspect something from the bits missing off the Roller and the fact that I strolled into breakfast next morning, so I'm told, still in my bib and tucker. Did the Fire-Brigade get to the Almshouses in time? I knew it was a mistake to ask Maurice's Chindit.

Nonetheless our little booze-up made me feel that there was after all something to be said for notching up the Three Score Years and Ten from which no traveller returns. The only other advantage I can think of is that it gives one a chance to cock a snook at the Gummers of this world who maintain that a hundred a day plus the firewater is certain death before thirty. Of course there are unlucky ones – Prosser-Cluff's brother springs to mind, not to mention P-C himself – whose system produces some chemical reaction with unpredictable results but as I said to the Boss on Sunday when she started waving her arms about in an exaggerated way to disperse the smoke between courses, 'Look at Winston. He was your hero. All this VE Day guff and so forth. If it hadn't been for the brandy bottle and fifty Corona Coronas a day we'd never have won the war. And he kept going till he was over ninety.' I could see a cloud pass over Margaret's brow as she envisaged the possibility of having me toddling about putting the foot in it for another twenty years. But she seemed to accept the logic of my argument.

I should say that this little contretemps sprang up during the official 70th Birthday luncheon at Chequers, graced by the presence of the boy Mark, plus yet another floozie, Howes, Mr Munster and the Corsican Twins. A far cry indeed from the good-natured bonhomie of the Frog and Loincloth. From the Boss's point of view, the highlight was the delivery of a wire from Hoppo congratulating 'The Duke of Thatcher' on being eighty.

Talking of which, the wrinkled cowboy seems to have got the bird on his Grand Absolutely Final Appearance Tour of Europe. His progress through the continental capitals reminded me very much of the monk on his peregrinations, with the egg-stalls doing a roaring trade and in one case, as he was about to address some bunch of big-noise wops, a pigeon being released, presumably

74

'. . . still in my bib and tucker . . .'

well dosed with laxative – a prank which reminded me very strongly of the time Reggie Stebbings employed the same device to clear a shareholders' meeting about to discuss the Chairman's expenses.

Needless to say I was far from being the main topic of conversation at my own seventieth birthday lunch. Almost as soon as Lady Howe had made her usual damnfool remarks about the charm of the floral arrangements, up spoke the Corsican Twins, embarking on an in-depth analysis of our failure at the polls in the Local Council Elections and the inroads made by the smarmy Doctor and his plonk-swilling Pinkos. To my astonishment, either Alberto or Luigi, I can never tell the difference, actually had the effrontery to lay the blame on the shoulders of the Boss. (I could only assume that Boris had laced his pre-lunch tomato juice with something a little more substantial.) At any rate his tongue was loosened and out he came with it: how her style was engendering consumer resistance and her packaging would have to be re-thought at a creative level. Not surprisingly our Italian friend got it clean between the eyes. How dare he say such a thing after they'd vetoed her Victory Parade at the end of the Miners' Strike, a mistake that had kept her awake night after night? If anyone was to blame for the polling figures it was Walker, a power-crazed financier manque who had waited till she was fighting for British jobs abroad before launching a cowardly attack on her. And now little Pym was organising his Private Army of wets. I had already heard this several times before, so I switched off, my thoughts reverted to the F & L, and the wonderful moment when Maurice did his gorilla on the overhead light and went through the stained glass window.

However, believe it or not, I tuned into the old girl doing her animal training act at Halitosis Hall a couple of mornings later, and it seemed our spaghetti-stained adviser's words had not fallen on entirely deaf ears. There was definitely a new note of pained condescension in her voice as she dismembered the wretched Welshman. But I am happy to say it didn't last long and when some yobbo caught her on the raw, the whip once more began to crack and he was soon up on his perch again licking his paws with his fellow chimps.

See you on VJ Night. God knows what they'll dredge out of the archives for that. I hope not the photograph of us and Prosser-Cluff in the fountains at Trafalgar Square kissing those Russian Lady Soldiers.

Onward into the Vale of Tears,

DENIS

1 JUNE 1985

Dear Bill,

I don't know if you've heard the joke Maurice picked up at the Club which is going the rounds about me? Question: 'What were Denis Thatcher's last words?' Answer: 'He didn't have any; his wife was with him to the end.' Quite amusing, I suppose, if you've had a few, which I had when I heard it from Maurice's lips, but looking at it written down it strikes me as being rather silly. Maurice says he sent it into Peterborough of the Daily Telegraph so you may have to read it again.

Entre nous, a certain amount of whistling in the dark has been going on here during the last week or so. Little Furniss who I had a snifter with in his office at the Nat-West really put the wind up me by saying that the big boys in the City are only waiting for the moment to what he calls 'go liquid'. I said I'd done that a long while ago, but he didn't seem to get the point. I don't think matters have been helped in the Square Mile by this Lloyds business. You probably heard about poor Ferdy Trapnell-Braine's missus, who had been drawing a very nice little couple of thou over the last few years, and suddenly got the buff envelope at the breakfast table saying she owed some Libyan Oiltanker man half a million quid. Ferdy says they'll have to sell their place in Majorca for a start, and he was even talking about making do with just one Roller instead of the three. Now they've brought in Lord Goodman to try and bale them out, though a more unsuitable person to drop into an over-crowded lifeboat it seems hard to imagine.

According to Furniss, the City Mob have finally come to the conclusion that Margaret is all gong and no dinner, largely because of the inflation rate taking an upturn. I haven't really dared tell M. this, but she has no one to blame but herself, allowing her fat friend at Number Eleven to jack up the price of everything in sight. What do they expect? Up till then, of course, beating inflation was the only feather in her cap, and now that's gone she's looking a bit thin on top. The hoi polloi seem to have reached the same conclusion at the same moment, and Moron, or

'. . . Little Furniss who I had a snifter with in his office . . .'

whatever they're called who do the opinion polls, came out with a real shocker, showing Kinnock and Steel neck and neck well out in front, with the Boss trailing along behind only a whisker ahead of Screaming Lord Sutch.

The only shot left in the Corsican Brothers' locker is to press full steam ahead with plans to put Halitosis Hall on TV every evening, the idea being that the punters will be impressed by the Grantham Gouger nightly throttling the wretched Ginger Nuts and tossing little Steel out of the ring like a piece of thistle-down, while the winos behind her bay and brawl. In my own view this scheme is doomed to failure, and may well be the end of democracy as we know it. As soon as Joe Public is allowed to lift up that particular rock and glimpse the slimy and disgusting creatures that infest the Palace of Westminster I would have thought it was only a matter of time before the Army had to be called in.

The only other scenario on the drawing board, an absolute non-starter, is the promised reshuffle in the Cabinet. However, despite heavy hints Hailsham is refusing to allow them to wheel him away, so force may have to be used to make him see reason. These geriatrics can be very obstinate, as you remember from all the trouble we had getting the Major's father to take down the barricades when he locked himself in the drinks cupboard at the Old Contemptibles. The Monk has also been letting it be known that a period of absolute rest in the House of Lords might be finally called for. But if you ask me any chances will be merely cosmetic, as the admen have it, and there isn't a hope in hell of shifting either little fuzzy-bonce Brittan or Matey Next Door.

The only laugh we've had has been Pym's little rebellion. A perfectly decent fellow, no doubt, but hardly the man to sound the trumpet call and bring Margaret's walls tumbling down. At the first feeble blast from his party squeaker all his followers were taken short and vanished over the horizon.

I got a belated birthday card from Rudolf Hess, extending his sympathy. Did I detect the Major's handwriting?

Yours for Life,

DENIS

79

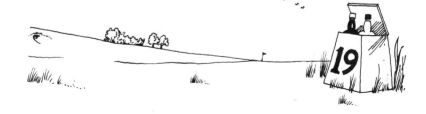